6.28-05

GUIDANCE
TO HEAVEN

*"It is appointed unto men once to die,
and after this the judgment."*
—Hebrews 9:27

D1562818

GUIDANCE TO HEAVEN

On the Catholic View of Life

By

Cardinal Giovanni Bona

Translated by

Fr. Andrew Byrne

Adapted for the modern reader by
Thomas A. Nelson

"For what doth it profit a man, if he gain the whole world, and suffer the loss of his own soul? Or what exchange shall a man give for his soul?"

—Matthew 16:26

TAN BOOKS AND PUBLISHERS, INC.
Rockford, Illinois 61105

The present edition of *Guidance to Heaven* is a careful adaptation for modern usage of Fr. Andrew Byrne's 1852 translation of Cardinal Giovanni Bona's *Manuductio ad coelum* (1658), published by James Duffy & Sons, London in 1881 (third edition) under the title, *The Hand that Leads to Heaven*.

Library of Congress Catalog Card No.: 95-60197

ISBN: 0-89555-520-4

Cover illustration (with adaptation) from *The Church's Year of Grace* (Vol. II), by Dr. Pius Parsch, copyright 1953 by The Order of St. Benedict, Inc. and published by The Liturgical Press, Collegeville, Minnesota. Used with permission.

Printed and bound in the United States of America.

TAN BOOKS AND PUBLISHERS, INC.
P.O. Box 424
Rockford, Illinois 61105

1995

"No man can serve two masters. For either he will hate the one, and love the other: or he will sustain the one, and despise the other. You cannot serve God and mammon."

—*Matthew* 6:24

PUBLISHER'S PREFACE

Guidance to Heaven by Cardinal Giovanni Bona was published in 1658 in Latin under the title *Manuductio ad coelum,* meaning literally, *"Guidance to Heaven."* It enjoyed wide popularity, going through fourteen Latin editions in forty years. It has been translated into Italian, French, English, German, Spanish and Armenian. The present translation was completed in 1852 under the title, *The Hand that Leads to Heaven,* and another English translation was published in London in 1900 under the title, *A Guide to Eternity.* The present English edition is adapted from the 1852 translation published by James Duffy & Sons, London in 1881 with the translator's original dedicatory introduction.

There Fr. Andrew Byrne, the translator, freely admits to having been very faithful to the original "and therefore more literal than perhaps some may wish," except that "the title alone, I may say, is the only part of the work not translated literally." Indeed, he seems to have taken his English title from the 1690 French translation of the book called *La Main Qui Conduit Au Ciel—"The Hand that Leads to Heaven."* One can see how this meaning can be derived from the Latin *Manuductio*, "the action of leading or guiding," but we have preferred to translate the title literally, just as the author named his Latin original. Fr. Byrne's translation has been adapted slightly for the present edition in order to make this wonderful little book more intelligible to the modern reader. We have deemed this necessary for five distinct reasons:

First and foremost, many of the English words used by the translator are no longer commonly used. We do not employ "strand" to mean "beach" or "seashore," or "meat" to mean "food," or "fly" to mean "flee," etc. Over forty such words have regularly been changed to their contemporary equivalents. *Secondly*, by the translator's own admission, he was "more literal than perhaps some may wish." This has led to some very unusual and convoluted expressions—which have been changed here to their obvious meanings. *Thirdly*, Latin is very compressed compared to English. Where the translator should have carried into English a more developed rendering, he instead transcribed certain passages in the original clipped style. These more developed translations have been given in this edition. *Fourthly*, Cardinal Bona was a very well read Latin scholar and a highly developed Latin stylist. One can detect in his writing some of the literary devices typical of many ancient pagan Latin writers—of whom Tacitus is probably the best example for conciseness because of the compressed meaning of many of his sayings. Where these literary devices have been carried over into English, we have generally "aired them out," that is, given the obvious fuller meaning of the translation in the interest of ease of understanding for the reader. And *fifthly*, Latin, as all students of that language realize, has no definite or indefinite articles ("the," "a" or "an"), which fact forces the reader of Latin to determine for himself whether the writer means, for example, "*the* man," "*a* man" or just "*man*." Where Fr. Byrne, in our judgment, missed interpreting these correctly, we have changed them to fit the obvious context.

All these minor enhancements considered, therefore, we can say that the present edition of *Guidance to Heaven* is "complete," for nothing has been excised, and it is "elucidated," rather than "unabridged," because meanings have been enhanced. For the most part, however, the present translation is exactly what Fr. Byrne rendered, which is according to him a very faithful translation of the original, but we believe the improvements made—which include modern, correct punctuation—dramatically enhance the meaning of this famous little book, for now there is no clumsiness or ambiguity left to distract the reader from its powerful message.

THE VALUE OF THE BOOK

The overriding value of *Guidance to Heaven* is the stark examination it makes of human life, and its exposure of the judgmental pitfalls that people commonly get into in assessing its nature. Most books of spirituality mention, and even dwell at length upon, the need for prayer, sacrifice, the Mass, the Sacraments, devotion to Mary, the Rosary, almsgiving, etc., to improve our lives and strengthen our wills for the battle we face in being good and saving our souls. Such books wax eloquent on Sanctifying Grace, the beneficence of God, man's miserable state, and so on.

In *Guidance to Heaven,* most mention of these important matters is left unstated, being understood and held as a backdrop to the general discussion. Rather, what the author addresses in this book is the entire Catholic attitude toward life—or, if you will, the Catholic philosophy of life! And this is no mean or trivial subject. Indeed, it is the foundation of all our spirituality, for out of the assessment we make of the nature of human life flow all our actions—as, for example, whether we attempt to go to Mass daily, receive the Sacrament of Penance weekly, pray the Rosary each day, practice True Devotion to Mary, tithe, give alms generously and so forth. From what do all these actions arise? They spring from our assessment of life and of the job we face in trying to save our souls. No other writer we know and definitely no other single book we have seen does such an admirable job of evaluating human life—of holding up to it a mirror, that we may see it as it really is—as does *Guidance to Heaven.*

Is this book better than *The Imitation of Christ,* or does it replace *The Spiritual Combat*—to both of which Catholic classics it has been compared? Hardly! On the other hand, does either of these singularly beneficial books perform anywhere near so well the essential function that *Guidance to Heaven* does in focusing our minds on the true Catholic attitude toward life? Not at all! A reading of *Guidance to Heaven* has the potential of transforming the entire orientation of a person's life. . .of causing conversions or reconversions to the Catholic Faith, of promoting vocations to the priesthood or religious life and of making serious Catholics out of the tepid. Truly, there is no other book we know quite like *Guidance to Heaven* for this remarkable contribution.

ABOUT THE AUTHOR

Cardinal Giovanni Bona (1609-1674) was born of an old French family at Mondovi in Piedmont (Italy). He became a Cistercian monk at Pignerola where, as later at Rome, he pursued study with great success. He worked for 15 years at Turin and was later prior at Asti and abbot at Mondovi. In 1651 he was called to preside over his entire congregation. Alexander VII made him Consultor to the Congregation of the Index and to the Holy Office, and in 1669 he was created Cardinal by Clement IX. After the death of this pope, many people thought that Cardinal Bona would succeed him to the Chair of St. Peter.

Cardinal Bona was renowned for his holiness, piety and scholarship. His best-known writings include *Via Compendii ad Deum—"A Short Way to God"* (1657); *Principia et documenta vitae Christianae—"Principles and Examples of the Christian Life"* (1673); *Manuductio ad coelum—"Guidance to Heaven"* (1658); *Horologium Asceticum—"The Ascetical Hour"* (c. 1674); *De Divina Psalmodia—"On Divine Psalmody"* (1663); *De Sacrificio Missae—"On the Sacrifice of the Mass"*; and *De Rebus Liturgicis—"On Liturgical Matters"* (1671).

This last is said to be a veritable encyclopedia of facts bearing on the Mass—such as rites, churches, vestments, etc. In summing up the Cardinal's many talents and virtues, Fr. Byrne quotes De Feller as saying: "To a profound erudition and vast knowledge of sacred and ecclesiastical antiquity, he united a piety as tender as it was enlightened." In short, Cardinal Giovanni Bona was a churchman of the first order—a monk, a scholar, an administrator, a writer, a "saint"—a man who, among other achievements, nearly became pope. Therefore, it was no small man and no mean pen that gave us *Guidance to Heaven*.

CONCLUSION

It is hoped that this fresh, new edition of *Guidance to Heaven* will effect in the hearts of its readers a profound realization of the shortness and uncertainty of human life, the length and unending nature of eternity—which constitutes our *true* life, if we save our souls—and those essential things that we must do to perfect ourselves so that we are certain, as much as is humanly possible, of a place in Heaven forever.

Thomas A. Nelson
February 10, 1995
Feast of St. Scholastica

CONTENTS

Contents

GUIDANCE TO HEAVEN

"And this I pray, that your charity may more and more abound in knowledge, and in all understanding: that you may approve the better things, that you may be sincere and without offence unto the day of Christ, filled with the fruit of justice, through Jesus Christ, unto the glory and praise of God."
—Philippians 1:9-11

Chapter I

THE END OF MAN

On the End of Man: The evil of departing from it and by what means and rule we arrive at it.

WHOSOEVER you are that read this book, I here propose to take you as by the hand to Heaven—that good indeed beyond whose possession you will desire nothing more. This is the scope, this is the end of all the sighs and desires of man. We all wish to be happy, but the greater part of mankind, on account of the darkness of Original Sin, leaving the true and Sovereign Good, apply themselves to the unprofitable pursuit of false and painted "toys." And these, indeed, thinking that the Sovereign Good consists in lacking nothing, have given this name to riches. Some, wishing to be rulers themselves or to be united to those in power, have considered the Sovereign Good to be the height of authority. Nay, others there are, who descending to the level of the basest objects and measuring the possession of the Sovereign Good by the chain which the flesh and its appetites have forged for them, esteem those most happy that wallow in pleasures. To such a low degree does their notion of beatitude sink. Thus toiling without fruit and as if wandering in a maze, the swifter they run after happiness, the farther they depart from it. They are therefore miserable because they know not their misery.

This is the subject, O unhappy man, that entangles you in great misfortunes because you desire indeed to live and die happily, but with regard to the nature of true happiness and the way of arriving at it, you are foolish and blind, being led astray by error, always winding into various delusions. All your actions, desires and contrivances are against yourself. For since your heart does not seek the things that are above, you do not bear in mind that Immense Good in which alone it ought to rest; but, like the creeping ants of the grove that in their empty career ascend to the highest tops of the trees and then descend to the roots, you too wander up and down without any fixed purpose. God, the Creator of all things, drew you out of nothing that you might love and serve Him alone with all your mind, with all your affection. For the same necessity which proves His existence establishes Him as your Last End. Ask yourself the serious question, what part of your life you devote to Him whose right to your whole being and every labor cannot be questioned. You err in your designs if you do not direct them to Him alone. For as the end of your journey is the place to which you are traveling and where you rest when you arrive, so the end of your being is God, to whom you ought to refer all your thoughts, words and deeds. So long as this Great Object is obtained, all your best wishes are crowned with the desired accomplishment, and everything that allures you away from this your Last End conducts you to eternal death.

As it happens when we are at sea, if leaving the vessel when it is brought to shore, you go to gather shells which the waves have cast upon the beach, your mind will always anxiously turn to the ship, lest the pilot call you; and as soon as he does, then forsaking all things else, you hasten back to the vessel. Thus you ought to act in the affairs of this life. Having your mind always fixed on God, use these external things in such a manner as not to allow them to cling to your heart nor to turn you away from the proposed end of your being. Those things serve *you* that *you* may serve God. Otherwise, falling away from the service of the one Divine Being, you shall be unhappily lost amid a multiplicity of useless things, and you shall worship as many idols as there are creatures which you love with disorderly affection. These are your gods, to which you sacrifice, not the ox or the goat, but by a base sacrilege you immolate yourself and your eternal salvation. The law of love does not suffer anything to be loved with God, unless in Him and for His sake alone. It is the ultimate of all misfortunes to turn away from the Sovereign Good through excessive attachment to creatures.

The prince of physicians says truly of unhealthy bodies that, where they are the more pampered, there they are the more injured by infection. The same must be said of souls steeped in vice. Wherefore, those who begin to forsake their evil habits must first of all cast out the poison of a bad life, and then the mind, having been purified, can taste the solid food of virtue. And this purification ought to be so perfect that all your sins should be atoned for, your affections for them put off, your evil habits torn up by the roots and your evil propensities and unruly appetites subjected to the calm empire of reason. The flesh too should be mortified—these things which are necessary for your physical needs should be reduced to just moderation, and a bridle placed on the tongue and senses. Finally, whatsoever throws an obstacle in your way, as you hasten up to the citadel of virtue, must be forthwith removed. Why do you tremble and fancy the path to eternal happiness to be difficult? It is in your power to make yourself happy, since He who is your first beginning and your Last End, sustains you; but you must leave yourself in order to come to Him, and the more remote your departure from yourself is, the nearer you approach to God.

It is necessary then, in the first place, that you set before your eyes the object of your desire and the End of your course; afterwards, you must closely inspect the way by which you ought to go to the possession of the Sovereign Good, not forgetting to notice the progress you make in it each day. And since it is in your power to become a different character from that which you have been, examine carefully your conscience, and opening your eyes, which have been blindly closed to your state, reflect seriously on what kind of person you *ought* to be. When on Judgment Day you shall not be able to avoid your delusion, it will *then* be too late to discover it. Learn *now* the remedy by which the impetuosity of your unlawful desires may be tamed and the just restraint that will hold within due bounds the vehemence of your excessive cares. Learn to disdain the things of earth and to withdraw your heart from those objects which cannot remain long with you; leave all things before they leave you, that when death comes, it may find nothing in you of which it can deprive you. Take then special care of your soul, in order that what by excellence ranks the *first* may not by negligence be left to the *last*. *"For what doth it profit a man, to gain the whole world, and suffer the loss of his own soul?"* (*Matt.* 16:26). Where the soul is lost there can be no gain.

Chapter II

THE NECESSITY OF A SPIRITUAL ADVISER

On the Necessity of a Spiritual Adviser: His character. The duties of the disciple.

NOTHING is more necessary for the person who begins to serve God than to put himself under the total guidance and instruction of some excellent master of the spiritual life. For who undertakes a journey in a strange land without a guide? Who learns a most difficult science without a tutor? You can count but few persons who, without the aid of anyone, have advanced themselves in virtue and arrived at a high degree of perfection. Maxims (which are necessarily formulated for universal practice) can be enjoined on the absent and handed down to posterity. But no one who is afar off shall be able to give counsel as to the time and manner in which certain things ought to be done, especially when we must hold a consultation in the presence of the things themselves. A physician cannot by letter prescribe the time when his patient is to take food and medicine; he must be there to "feel the pulse." The same thing happens in the salutary treatment of certain diseases of the mind, whose

symptoms are known only to him who is present with them. St. Paul, who had been chosen
to be the Doctor of the Gentiles, after his con-
version by Jesus Christ Himself, was sent to Ana-
nias that he might learn from him in person the
Christian way of life.

You undertook a hard and laborious task
indeed, when you applied yourself to the over-
coming of the malice of corrupt nature, to the
opposing the spirits of wickedness and, in defi-
ance of so many obstacles and impediments, to
forcing your way to the possession of virtue.
Wherefore, it is necessary for you to engage some
spiritual guide who will lend a helping hand,
point out the dangers, detect the snares and, in
this doubtful contest, show the way to victory.
But you say to me: "To whom shall I have
recourse?" A faithful and wise man who will be
both willing and able to help you, whom you
may venerate but not fear, who will rather amend
than punish your erring steps, and whose life
will speak more powerfully to your eyes than
his words to your ears. Commands will be poorly
received from him who preaches but does not
practice.

Select him for your guide who is a stranger
to flattery, one who disdains to mix in the rude
assembly of the popular crowd, who frequents
not the banquet halls of the rich nor the palaces
of princes, a man who may possess something
of great value in the guidance of life, as the
refiner does in the knowledge of gold. And as

the one can say, "Bring me any coin you wish and I shall discern its real value," so the other may say, "Bring me any affection of the heart, and I shall know how to pronounce on its merits." This man will apply fit remedies for driving away all the ills of the soul, as the skillful physician knows how to treat the maladies of the body, however hidden, and effect their cure. So highly gifted indeed ought to be this guide that he may be able to discern the inward motions of all the different spirits, fix landmarks between the virtues and vices, and benefit the morals of all: one who, diving skillfully into the deep recesses of your heart, may unfold those secrets which are known to none but God and yourself, and who himself being free from every evil affection, can devote himself to your spiritual welfare only. Having learned to detect and elude all the wiles and stratagems of Satan that led the soul astray, he will, in a feeling of leniency, teach and invite it back to God. Finally, let your spiritual guide be a person to whom you need not blush to lay open the hidden maladies of your soul and unlock the deep secrets of your heart. To be able to find a man blessed with these rare qualities will form no small portion of your happiness.

With this person you may at your leisure converse devoutly, submitting to his superior judgment all the evil inclinations and corrupt desires of your heart, all the good and all the evil you have done—in a word, whatsoever graces or favors you have received from God you may lay before him. Often beseech him to make known to you any irregular passion he may discover in you, and to do so frequently, lest prevented by the shame of reproving you, he hide your vices from you. But if he should say that he sees nothing in you deserving censure, do not think that you have escaped without blame, for his silence may arise from fear of your anger or despair of your amendment. But then urge and beseech him the more earnestly and show him by your actions how much you desire to improve. Begin to lay your faults before him and make your morals square with his admonitions. Be glad to receive reproach for your crooked ways, and you shall always return from him more healthy or curable in mind. Surrounded by so many evils as we are, it gives some hope of a cure for a person to be desirous of being healed.

The duties of the master and the disciple are mutual. The former must wish to impart instruction, the latter be anxious to profit by it. There is nothing to prevent the master from making the desired impression, except the unmanageable disposition and dullness of the disciple. Some indeed, relying on their own prudence, refuse to follow the guidance of another. "I know all you teach," they say. "Of what use is it to show us things self-evident?" Doubtless, it is of great use, for it sometimes happens that, although you know a thing, through inattention you do not pay heed to it. An admonition does not so much teach new things as awaken the memory to those which it has already learned, that it may retain them. The mind oftentimes seems to take no notice of things the most evident. Therefore, the knowledge of even these must often be impressed upon it. Besides, virtue receives new life when it is handled and driven forward. Some are held back by a shame that is puerile and unworthy of a man. Others there are who allow their misfortunes to prey inwardly on their own minds and, like lunatics observing a pernicious silence, are displeased with him who is bent upon their cure. Truly, it is the infernal enemy that suggests this unhappy silence, hoping thereby to bring certain destruction on the soul. You are not ashamed to expose the sores of the most delicate parts of the body in order to be cured; whereas, you studiously conceal the deadly cancers of the soul—as if to hide them were the same thing as to heal them—although it may be almost impossible but that they will reveal themselves even against your will. But he who conceals his wounds shall never obtain a cure.

Can your physician do you any harm when he makes your hidden maladies known to you and says: "You are in danger. . .You are ill...You have a fever. Today you must abstain from food and drink nothing but water." On the contrary, you praise him and return him thanks as for a kindness received. But if anyone should say: "Your passions are like the raging sea... Your ideas are vain... Your affections are irregular," then presently you exclaim: "Oh what a heinous crime! It is one that deserves to be punished with a bloody sword! Oh insult not to be born! Unhappy man!'' What harm can the adviser, anxious for your salvation, do you? It is true that the mirror which he holds up before you exhibits your deformity—that it declares your real state. Correct, therefore, all that he reproved; improve your morals, wash away your stains. You can easily, if you wish, present yourself blameless to the eyes of the whole world.

Chapter III

PURIFICATION FROM SIN

On Purification from Sin: Affection towards sin must be put off and vice destroyed. No remedy is more effectual for overthrowing vice than the consideration of death and eternity.

WHEN MAN commits sin, he strays from the Happy End of his being, and this straying is the cause of all his misfortunes. From this evil seed springs every pain; with this deadly poison the entire world is infected. This evil is not perceived until sin is committed, but as soon as you are guilty of it, you are given to understand into what a great misfortune you have fallen. There have been tyrants who have bound the carcasses of the dead to living persons to torment them with the horrid stench. A similar punishment attends sinners. They are, as it were, chained to their torments, nor can they find a place where they may flee from them. Unless you suffer the loss of some "supposed good" in order to prevent sin, great shall be your sufferings in consequence of having committed it. A sinful deed is scarcely conceived in the mind when it is in labor with its own punishment. This punishment in turn becomes the parent of death, to which

the fiery offspring of pain and then Hell itself
succeed. The conscience, therefore, must be
thoroughly purified by the beneficial influence
of contrition, Confession and satisfaction. We
must avoid not only the more grievous sins, but
even the least and lightest faults which, although
they do not bring death to the soul, dissolve its
energies by degrees and prepare it for a mortal
stain. When the ship is lost and sunk in the deep,
it is of little moment whether it was one great
wave or the water stealing into it drop by drop
through our neglect that caused its destruction.
In proportion to the facility with which these
minor faults may be avoided, so their stains on
your morals are of darker shades of guilt. The
weaker the enemy is, the greater the disgrace
if you be vanquished by him.

Unless you put off every affection for sin, however small, you shall never be able to implant
virtue in your soul and reinstate yourself in your
original liberty. You should not be like the Isra-
elites, living with your body indeed in the desert, but having your thoughts in Egypt. You are
going on in an evil course if, after the pardon
of sin and the relinquishment of your base
desires, you still lend an ear to vile conversation
and are charmed with perishable beauty. Truly
you ought to tear up by the roots your vices and
bad habits which, after the pardon of their guilt,
remain as the unhappy offspring of sin. If you
cut off the branches only, the untouched roots
will still sprout forth young shoots of iniquity.

You say indeed that you wish to destroy your vices. It is false, for you do not altogether close the door against them, but content yourself in opposing them. You say that you are displeased with your base manner of living. I believe you, for who does not feel his bleeding wounds? Sinners hate and love their vices at the same time, and they detest them even at the moment they indulge in them. But to what purpose do you condemn your sins by your words if you embrace them by your deeds? There is no sinner so profligate who is not sometimes disgusted with his vices, although he may be soon reconciled to them again. But he who is truly converted to God lays the axe to the root and thus destroys the minutest fibers of his vices. Then, mindful of his great weakness, he most carefully avoids all the occasions of sin, and full of holy terror, he recoils from and shudders at the very shadow of evil.

Why do you in vain sit unresolved and excuse yourself to God over the frailty of nature, who orders the complete destruction of your vices? No one knows the measure of your virtues better than God, who has liberally bestowed them on you. Why, therefore, do you not presently obey, since it is not the advantage of Him who commands but the interest of him who obeys that is sought in the Divine Law? Oh blind and impious rashness! Fired by a malice like that of a slave, you audaciously fly in the face of God and say that it is hard to obey Him, as if indeed He imposed commandments upon you which you could not bear, so that He would seem thereby to have sought your punishment and not your salvation. Truly this is human perversity! To pretend that you gain nothing but evil at the hands of God and that pains alone are the end of His commandments. But if you will bring to the test the powers with which He has endowed you, it will become apparent that you can do much more than you imagined. The conflict in itself is not difficult, but the difficulty is your lack of courage to engage in it. Many things which at first wore a terrifying aspect have been by a little experience turned into laughter. Only make a beginning, and you shall not disparage your best effort. God does not desert His own soldiers, and in this perilous warfare your forces will be in exact proportion to the intensity of your desire of serving Him.

You shall easily overcome every vice if you shall each day persuade yourself that now the sun shines upon you for the last time. What is it that chains you to this earth? The unhappy absence of the thought that you must be quickly torn from it. Dead bodies are daily carried before your eyes to the grave, which forces even him who is unmindful of his mortality to reflect upon death. But you walk through the very midst of the carnage which death is causing around you, and still you think less of death than of anything else, and though there is nothing you see more frequently than death, there is nothing you more quickly forget. But a day will come at last that will dissipate the dullness which has unhappily clouded your mind and that will remove you far from that activity which has bound you to your bodily appetites. Let the blindness which has so long held your eyes be driven away, and then when you shall behold the light, you shall know the darkness in which you have lived. Out of so many years which you have spent, produce, if you can, one single day devoted to solid virtue—one day not stained by any sin. Your untaught years shed their blossoms amid silly play and childish sports; your childhood in foolishness and wantonness; your headlong youth perhaps in crimes and wickedness. After so many years that have passed from your cradle to your gray hairs, nothing now remains but the bitter fruit of sin. Alas! What distress will come upon you when the dark remembrance of past sins will make you blush with shame and the dark prospect of the future terrify you! What will it then profit you to have heaped up so much wealth by the sweat of your brow and to have watched over it by so many cares? What shall all the shameful delights of flesh and blood avail you? What advantage shall you draw from all the empty titles of honor—from the purple* and the crown? Oh, if you were allowed to return to the playthings of childhood and begin anew

---

* Purple was the color worn by kings and royalty in the ancient world. —*Publisher,* 1995.

to weave the web of life over again, doubtless it would be woven with a better and a finer texture. But in that last fatal moment, those fine vows you made shall have been made in vain. If then you wish to make the best use of time, begin now to do so, and forsake those things which you will then wish to have forsaken. It can be no great sacrifice to renounce these momentary things in order to gain those that are eternal.

If you could converse with the dead and ask them what they think of their past lives, scarcely would you find one whose ideas of riches, honors and vanities were not infinitely different from those which he had entertained when upon earth. Beyond the grave, all things are weighed on a fairer scale and valued as they deserve. The wisdom learned by sinners only in death is indeed wisdom learned too late, but you may profit much from their woeful example, by learning to correct your own errors. You are now able to pass in safety through the ocean of time; why do you wait for the storm? In the present relative prosperity you can save yourself from the impending calamity; why do you procrastinate, toying over the extreme danger of falling into it? When you are already sunk in the waves, your care comes too late to save you. That prudence which finds you have already perished comes too late for your redemption. How many great and holy men, forsaking themselves and the world and all things which might be opposed to their progress in virtue, have applied themselves to this business alone, *viz.*, to learn how to live and to die? However, not a few have left this life confessing that they did not as yet know themselves, so difficult is it to learn this knowledge. But are you putting off the execution of wise counsels until white-haired old age and wish to begin to live for God at that late period of life, to which relatively few ever arrive? It is great folly indeed to fancy you can then begin to live when in fact you must die.

O most imprudent of all men, into what abyss do you precipitate yourself? You believe these things, and you live as if you did not believe them. Your time here is but the passing of a shadow; your life a mere point; and if there can be anything found less than this, to that it may be likened. Scarcely are you born when you cease to live. Just try to cause even one day to stand still, to prevent one hour only from passing on, to stop even for a moment the march of time. In vain do you make the attempt, for time will sooner transport you with itself than it will cease to fly on the swiftest of wings, hurrying you and all things into ruin. Is it for this present moment that you lay aside an eternity which shall never end? Oh folly! Oh blindness! For a body which shall soon perish you never cease to toil and provide all those things which belong to it, without placing any bounds to your treasures for its welfare, but you bestow no care on the laying up of good things for your immortal soul in *"the ages to come,"* as if that soul did not belong to you! Your body is ill, and you undergo every danger to restore it to health; your soul languishes in sin, and you neglect it and do not feel for its maladies! When was it said to you, "Go to sea, lest you die," and you delayed? When was a most bitter medicine presented to you, and you refused to take it? God orders you to do very easy things in order that you may live eternally, and you do not wish to obey Him! If you should be involved in a legal case, all your conversation, all your thoughts are engaged about it, lest you fail to prepare the due assistance, hoping that the judge may pass sentence in your favor. But the Last Judgment is pending, on which rest the sorrows or joys of eternity, and you laugh, trifle, and sin—which will damn you forever! Ah, put an end to your madness, and rising from the abyss of your vices, keep your conscience every day in such a state as it ought to be in at the last moment of your life. Behold true philosophy, to lead the soul as much as possible away from the body and to separate their interests from each other.

To betake yourself to flight from time and immerse yourself in eternity ought to be your chief business, your recreation, your labor, your rest. All things that pass under the laws of eternity become fixed and unchangeable forevermore. The avaricious glutton, after so many ages in Hell, still asks for one drop of water and shall continue with eternal moans to ask for it in vain.

Eternity is a duration always present, which cannot be named without deep sighs and feelings of terror. It is a wheel always turning, perpetual, boundless, and always beginning anew. The serious thought of eternity mixes wormwood with the false delights of the world and casts men down with fearful sadness, as if struck by lightning from Heaven. This thought overcomes the rebellious spirit—lulled to rest in the bosom of fruitless cares—and awakens it to the practice of virtue; it gives a relish to hunger and thirst, making every labor easy, every sorrow sweet, every pain abound in comfort, while it tells the child of sorrow to weep not, that all these things are only momentary. Let the mighty space of the heavens, which extend to immensity on all sides, be filled up with figures. Who but God alone shall be able to count this almost infinite series of numbers? However, this countless multitude of ciphers cannot express the beginning of eternity! As many years, as many ages as there are units in the numbers above shall pass away, and as yet eternity suffers no diminution! As yet those most unhappy mortals who are tormented in the endless fire of Hell have not come to the beginning of their eternity of despair. Oh harder than any rock must be your heart if considerations like these cannot make you quiver for fear and move you to a serious amendment of your life!

Chapter IV

GLUTTONY

*On Gluttony: Its evils and remedies, and by what
signs we know it is overcome.*

AS GLUTTONY affords nourishment to the
other vices, your first contest must be to
overthrow it. Gluttony it was that first made us
subject to the death of both soul and body, for
our first parents, by eating the forbidden fruit,
have bequeathed death to all men, even before
they imparted to them life. And now our spiritual
enemies make use of the same vice, that by thus
weakening and enervating our forces, they may
throw us down and trample us underfoot. This
vice is the parent of an unhappy progeny, *viz.*,
dullness, faintness, weariness, scurrility, talkativeness, dissoluteness, impurity, quarrels and
contentions. Finally, gluttony gives birth to stu-
pidity of mind and brings on the ruin of all virtues, the waste of property, squalid poverty, a
long series of ailments and in the end death itself,
prematurely hastened by an overloaded stomach.
Among the infirm, few can be found whom gluttony has not allured onward to the destruction
of their health, for if the body be not afflicted
by those noxious dispositions arising from an

excess of food and drink, it may indeed be attacked by disease, but it cannot be easily subdued. Gluttony has cut down more men than the sword.

Oh most vile servitude of the body! Oh cupidity that can never be satisfied! Nature has given you a small body; however, you surpass in greediness the largest and most voracious animals of the world. A few acres of pasture satisfy the bull, and one forest feeds many elephants, but the universe is too little for you; your gluttony thirsts after every bird that flies in the air, every fish that swims in the water and every species of game that can find cover in the woods. Go into the kitchens of the great and behold the cooks busy before several fires and the sweat pouring down the faces of the crowd of male and female servants; see the great number of animals slaughtered and the cellars gorged with wine; observe the great care with which the attendants arrange the silver cups and the skill they display in the laying of the dishes and plates on the table, as well as in carving the fowl. Behold, in short, the quickness they show in waiting on the company. You can scarcely believe that it is for only one family that the wines of so many vintages and kingdoms are uncorked and such crowded tables are prepared. I do not want you to deprive yourself of the nourishment necessary for you; the appetite is obstinate in its demands for daily food, nor can it be overcome; but here lies concealed a most artful snare of concupiscence by which the soul is oftentimes entangled, for under the pretext of necessity, the most extravagant waste takes place so that one may indulge in bodily pleasure. Do you wish to know the small quantity of food that banishes hunger? Take into calculation that you are but one person only; measure the size of your body and consult your appetite, and you shall see that any excess which goes beyond your just measure is not necessary. Nature is satisfied with little, but luxury demands an immensity.

Hunger, in its demands, is not at all ambitious. Provided it has a sufficiency, it craves nothing more. The taste, having obtained its momentary gratification, finds the sumptuous repast not more agreeable to it than the homely fare. If you be hungry, you must eat; if thirsty, you must drink. But nature is not concerned whether the bread be made of the coarsest meal or the finest flour, whether the water, cooled artificially by mountain snow, be brought from a neighboring brook or from a great distance; all that nature demands is that its hunger be satisfied and thirst quenched. The fishes caught in the sea, rivers and lakes; the birds taken on the wing; the game killed as they wildly pass through the woods; the different kinds of wine and all the various sauces of Apicius are but the torments by which unhappy luxury punishes itself. Epicurus himself praises a life of temperance as the one most pleasurable, for there is no food so sumptuous which nausea does not render insipid, none so tasteless that hunger does not make sweet. Do you wish to cast aside all superfluous care for food and drink? Reflect on death, that you shall soon die and that the body which you have pampered by so great a variety of delicious banquets shall itself become the banquet of worms. Consider well, then, for whose feast you fatten yourself and that you ought to support the body in such a manner as not to injure the spirit. If you use wholesome food—which is easily obtained and met with everywhere—you shall injure neither your budget nor your health. To be well disciplined as to the use of the plainest food is a great part of human happiness. We have never been able to understand how superfluous many things have been until they begin to fail us. The body needs nourishment, but not a variety of rich delicacies.

But you should not flatter yourself for having disdained superfluous things. Then only do you deserve praise when you make no account of those things which are even necessary, when you shall have persuaded yourself that common bread and a little wine, not strong or mixed with water, suffice for food and drink, when you shall have learned that vegetables grow not only for the beast but for man also. Then indeed shall I admire you, when in the taking of your daily food, you shall have nothing in view but the necessity you are under of sustaining your natural powers and doing all for the glory of God; when you shall have disdained the rich banquets and tables of the great, going with reluctance to your own table to take your repast, somewhat like a patient taking his medicine; when you shall have studied to bridle the pleasure of taste and taken care to mortify it, as it cannot be altogether removed; when, obliged by indisposition, you shall only with regret have taken more delicate food; finally, when you shall be possessed of perfect purity of body and spirit, for the evidence of true abstinence is found not in the weakened state of the body, but in the perfection of chastity; when you have arrived at such a state, then indeed shall I admire you!

Chapter V

IMPURITY

On Impurity: How base this vice is; how easy it is to fall into it, and how it is to be avoided. We must follow the solid pleasures of the mind.

THERE IS NO vice more filthy than impurity, none at whose commission we ought to feel blushes of a deeper red. The Apostle has declared that the bare mention of this vice carries infamy with it, teaching that it should *"not be so much as named among"* Christians. (Cf. *Eph.* 5:3). Hence arises that shame which all upright men are wont to feel should they doubt that any sin of impurity, which they might have once committed, had come to the knowledge of another person; hence, some unfortunate penitents conceal from the minister of Christ in the most sacred tribunal of Penance the errors of that slippery age in which few are out of harm's way, choosing to undergo everlasting torments and ignominy after death rather than submit to only an imaginary disgrace in this life. But the unhappy man who is buried in the filthy mud of this vice scarcely ever arises from it. His salvation seems given up for lost who is infected by this plague, for what can human efforts do against a vice so formidable? No one can be chaste except the person on whom God bestows this angelic gift.*

The first remedy for this disorder, therefore, is fervent prayer to God, that He Himself, who alone holds dominion over us, may heal and preserve us. Then it is necessary to resist impure thoughts at their very approach—and with the same promptitude to which you would be excited in casting a burning coal from your garments. Woe to you if you once give yourself up to deliberate reflection on even the least thing regarding this vice. That fortress is very near to surrender whose governor begins to hold familiar conversation with the enemy. We must carefully avoid, likewise, every occasion of sin arising from idleness, gluttony, impure contact of any kind and the company of the wicked; nor must we neglect any precaution in this awful struggle. There are even among the pious some remains of this vice, which must be altogether extirpated. These are certain

---

* The meaning of the author is obviously that no one can attain to purity without the help of God, but obviously, with the help of God, all people can achieve this virtue. Scripture says, "My grace is sufficient for thee." (2 *Cor.* 12:9). And again, "I can do all things in him, who strengtheneth me." (*Phil.* 4:13). And again, "Is it my will that a sinner should die, saith the Lord God, and not that he should be converted from his ways, and live?" (*Ezech.* 18:23). The author's meaning is clearly that the inordinate lure of this faculty in man will lead a soul to perdition if he or she does not call upon the supernatural help of God to overcome impure thoughts and actions. —*Publisher,* 1995.

puerile affections and attachments which, although they may not be evil in themselves, may well be compared to the hissing of the hidden serpent before it emits the fatal poison, so that these are the first enchanting preludes by which the mind, by means of the senses, yet without perceiving it, becomes allured and falls a prey to sin, if you do not immediately withdraw yourself from these preludes. You shall never be great in virtue if you despise these little things; from small beginnings great things take their rise.

You must in the first place be on your guard lest too much confidence in yourself deceive you. The man who does not tremble for his own frailty has already fallen. Many and great have been the men who—after their confessions and victories, their signs and wonders—have, by one unguarded glance at a female, tumbled down to utter ruin. I need not here mention the examples of *Samson, David* and *Solomon,* which have so often been solemnly recited. There are others of recent date and which daily occur, and should even other examples not be immediately at hand, you yourself have in your own bosom shameful evidence of your weakness, from which you may learn not to be high-minded, but to fear. Amid so much evidence from all ages and nations, is it not extreme madness to presume on one's own strength and not avoid the danger of sin? But this incredulity belongs to human obstinacy, *viz.,* never to believe that others have fallen, until it sees that itself has perished. God has made woman the companion of man, but by the deceit of the Serpent she can easily assume a hostile position. In her fallen state can be found all that may strike, wound, burn and destroy; if she be corrupted, or even careless, then no hyena, no basilisk can vie in danger with her voice and eyes. Ah, whosoever you are, if you desire your salvation, flee all unchaste glances and conversation with a woman. She still retains that tempting nature which has banished man from Paradise and woefully exercises its influence to this very day.*

---

* These remarks of Cardinal Bona are to be understood as applicable only to a certain class of the female sex, not all; and in this limited sense they are indeed as true as they are severe. But, doubtless, he did not mean to imply that these remarks are not equally applicable to many among the male sex, for has not the "deceit of the serpent" affected one as much as the other? Alas! Sad experience alone demonstrates this truth. The temptations, dangers and hostilities arising from the social intercourse of both sexes may therefore be fairly divided between them. In these there is no monopoly for either. Both in a woeful degree are tempters and destroyers.

But in the kingdom of grace we almost forget the effects of our fallen nature. "Oh happy fault [of Adam] that deserved such and so great a Redeemer"—St. Augustine. Jesus Christ has made us *"co-heirs"* of His glory. Through *Mary*, then, we have risen to a position among the celestial spirits, infinitely more sublime than that from which, through *Eve*, we had unhappily fallen in Paradise. *Her all nations call blessed.* And who can number those angelic multitudes of her sex who imitate her virtues, "to whose eternal sighs the Church in all ages is indebted," and whom St. Augustine justly calls, "The devout female sex."—*Translator.*

It is usual to make on this subject many excuses of necessity, custom and pure intention, but under these fair appearances great misfortunes are found lurking, for out of these pretenses sally forth harmful liberties, unguarded conversations, light behavior, neglect of modesty, keepsakes frequently interchanged and certain jokes, all of which by degrees overthrow shame, and in the end destroy all becoming bashfulness. These actions gain strength with time, and he who in the beginning blushed at the approach of a woman, will afterwards, with unchanged countenance, behold lascivious eyes and naked breast, while the agreeable poison makes its way to his heart and he is lost before he even perceives his danger. Thus the eye of reason by degrees becomes dim and in the end quite blind. In this way the soul that is created for Heaven, becoming forgetful of God and of itself, is chained down to the earth, until the flame of concupiscence is swallowed up in that fire which shall never end. Oh unhappy mortals, whose filthy and momentary pleasures come to so mournful an end! One would think that all these men have eaten the Sardonic herb, as they laugh even in the face of death.

O insane man! You have no counsel of your own to direct you, and you desert that of another. What do you seek? Pleasures? God has laid up those in store for you in Heaven—such indeed as shall never fade. Do you wish to enjoy the false pleasures of this world and to be excluded from those that are eternally enjoyed in Heaven? Where is your reason? Where is your prudence? Look up to Heaven and all its blissful citizens. In bygone times they mingled their bread with ashes and their drink with tears. You might have seen them oppressed on all sides with the troubles of this world, always in a sad and rueful state, always bathed in tears, always vigilant in prayer, and far away beyond the joys of this world; they made their way, nonetheless, through instruments of torture, swords and persecution to the kingdom of Heaven. Behold, on the other hand, Hell and the troops of the damned, lost in despair and buried in flames dark and eternal. These once enjoyed the false delights of this world and all the charms and pleasures of the flesh, but now, too late, they know how woefully those enjoyments have injured their immortal souls. Reflect seriously on these truths, and if you have faith, tremble with horror. That which delights here has only one moment's duration, but that which torments hereafter endures forevermore.

But if you wish for pleasure even in this life, why do you not seek rather for that true and solid pleasure which is as pure as it is immutable and which arises from a well-ordered mind, so that you may become a subject of joy to yourself? The pleasure of the flesh is fading, fragile, false—always drunk with wine, scented with perfumes and full of fears lest it be discovered; its favorite haunts are in places given to debauchery and good cheer and therefore doomed to censure. That pleasure may glitter on the outside, but it is tortured by pains within it; it is extinguished as soon as it begins and perishes in the very exercise of its own function. But the pleasure of the mind is tranquil, noble, insurmountable, always secure and constant, a stranger to weariness and regret; no shame awaits it, no grief pursues it, while it never forsakes its possessor. If you desire to enjoy this angelic pleasure, you must subdue all the allurements of the flesh. It is indeed true pleasure to disdain all earthly pleasure.

Chapter VI

AVARICE

On Avarice: Its malice; a comparison between the rich and the poor; the deceit and vanity of riches.

SUCH is the malice of avarice that it hides itself in so secret a manner that we can find no one who will confess he is guilty of it. This you ought to know, lest you be deceived by it. This man heaps up riches as a provision for himself and his family; that man does the same, consulting for the interests of the poor; and another, that he may redeem himself from his past sins by deeds of generosity. But not one of these would distribute the treasures which he has amassed. On the contrary, they heap fresh sums of gold upon those already accumulated, and in the interim, life hastens to a close. And as the thirst of the sick person cannot be quenched by the water of the pleasant stream (which he may even stir with his hand) until he moves his lips to it and drinks the refreshing draft, so the cursed thirst for gold cannot be satisfied with anything because riches and treasures cannot really find their abode in the heart of the avaricious man, where only the immoderate love of them can reside. God alone can satisfy the human soul, whose capacity cannot be filled but by Him only.

O avaricious man, fortune may transport you far beyond the opulence of Solomon, possessing all those riches which the wealthy in past ages have heaped together; you may cover your land with marble, your walls with gold and your roofs with gems. You may not only possess riches, but even walk upon their superabundance. To this add statues, pictures and all that art in the service of luxury has wrought. From the possession of all these things you shall only learn to desire even greater treasures. The desires arising from nature have their bounds, but those springing from mere fancy—false in itself— are infinite. To what purpose do you possess money in your coffers and corn in your granary if you do not take into account what you have already laid up in them, but keep your mind tortured with the thought of all you have as yet to acquire? He is in need of the whole world whom even the world cannot satisfy. But would to God that you would reflect on the great evils that riches bring with them and the immense good of which they deprive you! Doubtless you would then learn how true those words of the Apostle are: *"For the desire of money is the root of all evils."* (*1 Tim.* 6:10). This is the infernal source in which frauds, wars, perjuries and treacheries take their rise. Remove avarice, and there is an end to discord; let this vice cease, and ambition is no more. Avarice it is that fills the land with thieves, the sea with pirates, cities with riots, families with deceits and courts of law with injustice. Truly there is a strange alliance—even in name—between riches and all the vices.

Draw a comparison, if you will, between the rich and the poor who lives content. Behold the countenances of both: the one, full of rude cares, betrays the troubled workings of his mind; the other, by his serene looks, shows the true joy of his spirit. The slight tinsel happiness of the former glitters only amid those vexations which corrode his heart. The mind of the latter, devoid of grief, enjoys the sweets of internal peace. The rich man, torn with anxious cares to make more money, and perplexed with fears lest he lose what he has already amassed, is exposed to all the injuries of fortune and is therefore most miserable, for the more he has, the more he desires to have. On the contrary, the poor man is most rich in his poverty, desiring only what is necessary and fearing nothing, as he is attached to nothing that can be taken from him. Oh, how joyous the days, how calm the nights that mark the career of the poor man! But the rich man, like one surrounded by thorns, feels anguish of mind wheresoever he turns, which makes him sick at heart. He slumbers spiritually, however, in a deadly stupor, since he is insensible to those things which threaten the life of his soul.

Hear a lesson, O miserable man, whose avarice cannot be satisfied. Your mansion-houses may in all places dazzle the spectator, your treasures may be immense, your possessions may extend beyond the sea; a day, however, will come—a day fixed from all eternity to be your last—when, with a mind as bitter as it will be unwilling, you must forsake all these things and your very life. They shall all vanish, all perish, and on their account you yourself shall perish forever. Then at last you shall understand how much those things ought to be disdained which you now admire. In this you resemble little children, who place much value on all that amuses them. They are delighted when they find little pebbles of divers colors on the seashore. You are still more foolishly in love with ingots of gold and precious stones. I do not say that you should renounce riches if God has poured them into your hands, but that your riches should not be taken from another nor obtained with sordid gain, solicitude or superfluous care. You may receive them into your house, but not into your heart, and you should be ready to lose them when it is the will of God that you should become poor. He is truly rich who has no need of riches. You should not wait until the thief or some accident takes your possessions from you; do their work beforehand, and deprive yourself of that which may fall into the hands of others, you yourself becoming indifferent to all outward things. You shall be truly in possession of them if you regard these things as not belonging to you.

Endeavor to remove far from you all pomp and ostentation and to adjust your food and apparel, not to the customs of the world, but to a Christian life. The practice of frugality will teach you how to change poverty into riches. Nature desires but little—*viz.*, not to feel hunger, thirst or cold. You need not purchase rich marble to build a house for yourself nor carry on a trade with the extremities of the earth to clothe yourself. And why can you not quench your thirst without a cup wrought in gems and crystals, which mingles the fear of breaking it with the pleasure of drinking out of it? Shall not your knife be able to cut your bread unless the handle be made of ivory or enriched with pearls? Why can you not wash your hands in an earthen basin? Cannot your lamp afford you light unless it be the work of some ingenious hand? He is indeed a slave to gold who fancies he must make it serve his pomp. How much more useful would it be to love those true riches which make a man better and of which neither the changes of fortune nor even death itself can rob us. Why do you fear poverty, which purchases a perfect kingdom in your heart? *"The kingdom of God is within you."* (*Luke* 17:21). Oh may it be far from you to seek any other good! Seek this, your only good. *"None is good but God alone."* (*Luke* 18:19). Behold Him who is your possession and your kingdom, in whom all goods and all treasures are concentrated. The world seems as nothing to him to whom God is all things.

Whatsoever appears to shine and to be great in the world is a phantom, vain and deceitful;

it is nothing. Why are you in admiration when
you see a man clothed in gold and purple and
surrounded by a great troop of servants? It is all
vain pomp. All these things make a great display,
but are not real possessions; and while they please
the eye, they pass away like a shadow. I have
learned this truth, not from the schools of ancient
philosophy, nor from the Cross of Christ, nor from
the eternal wisdom of God, but from the world
itself and the slaves of its vanities. Hear Aman,
whom riches, power and honors had elevated
above all the men of his time. He assembled his
friends and declared to them that all these things
were nothing. *"I think,"* said he, *"I have nothing, so long as I see Mardochai the Jew sitting
before the king's gate."* (*Esther* 5:13). Oh mock-
ery! Oh blindness! Often have I read and often
heard that all these things, when compared with
the goods which virtue brings forth and eternity
nourishes, are nothing. But these earthly goods
are brought down to a still lower level: when compared with their own nothingness, they seem to
be nothing. Therefore your labors are worth nothing if you do not disdain the nothingness of these
things. It is necessary to disdain whatsoever is
in you which may have the effrontery to pretend
to be something. You must bind in chains and
trample down your covetousness and accustom
yourself to the practice of poverty and to esteeming things according to their utility. You shall easily disdain all these things if you always remember
that you shall soon die.

Chapter VII

ANGER

On Anger: The character of a man in anger; its effects, causes and remedies.

I AM angry with anger itself. Other than righteous indignation, there is no just anger but that which is directed against this rabid and hateful monster—a passion so outrageous and turbulent that when it once seizes upon the heart of man, it leaves in him scarcely a vestige of human nature. Anger is a sort of brief madness; it cannot govern itself and thirsts for arms, blood and punishments. Thoughtless of all decency and unmindful of friendship, it rushes upon another with dangerous weapons to inflict an injury; it resembles very much those ruins of things which are broken to pieces on the spot where they fall. All beauty forsakes the angry man. The eyes become, as it were, on fire and aflame; the veins are swollen, the hair stands on end, the lips tremble, the teeth gnash, the mouth foams and the voice distends the throat with furious denunciations. There is no passion by which man externally seems so much disturbed. By it the countenance is deformed, the forehead contracts, the head shakes, the feet stagger, the hands tremble and the whole body is agitated, being violently carried here and there by the indecent motion of this passion. Add to all this the threatening gestures of the angry man—his clenched fists, his stamping on the ground, his beating his breast, tearing his hair, rending his garments—while his blood "boils" from his heart through all his arteries and veins. Who shall be able to describe the state of his soul whose outward image is so deformed? You may fancy you see those monsters which the poets formerly described as inhabitants of Hell when you behold a man in anger; for those are pictured to us as surrounded with flames, encompassed by serpents and roaring so loud with dire moans as to make even the demons themselves tremble.

Such may be said to be the state of the angry man—bloody, outrageous, cruel—and his mild nature lost in the mad ferocity of a wild beast. We can hide the motions of the other passions and cherish them in secret, but anger shows itself externally, and like a raging fire, consumes all before it. The more you strive to conceal it, the more it rises over all bounds. He who abandons himself to this passion sets no limits to his fury, nor does he allow anything to restrain him.

Moreover, the other vices are restrained within certain bounds, but there is no place of refuge from the violent assaults of anger. Its insolence would dare advance to Heaven itself. Behold in this the bitter source from which flow those torrents of blasphemies and murmurings and those disputes of the impious concerning the providence of God. Indeed, we are so ingenious in providing fuel for our vices that we are not only angry with those who are supposed to have injured us, but even the thought of some future injury is enough to irritate us, and we look upon it as already inflicted on us, although there may be no foundation whatever for it, save in our own imagination.

Often we are angry although we do not know the object of our anger; and where there is no other object against which we can vent our rage, we turn it against ourselves. We even suffer our fury to explode upon the loving heads of those who do not even have it in them either to offend or reproach us, which shows that it is not an injury alone that may excite our anger. Thus, we often rend our garments, smash our belongings on the ground, break our pens and tear our paper when we cannot use these according to our particular fancy. Thus, we feel angry at a cup misplaced, a table badly laid, a servant not sufficiently quick, the noisy movement of a seat and many other things which neither deserve nor feel our anger. In like manner we are angry with a hard-mouthed horse, a dog barking, little birds fluttering, flies playing importunately around us or gnats biting us—which is quite enough to make them suffer the punishment of our impatience. See the excess of your madness! You inflict punishment on inanimate nature and the brute creation, which in reason ought rather to have chastised your mad fits of anger.

If you wish to see the effects of anger and the train of evils which it draws after it, you shall find that there is no pestilence so destructive to the human race; you shall behold the carnage of men, women and children, the overthrow of cities, and whole nations brought to ruin. You shall behold that plague created by human hands and, in the broad scope of its work in history, immense heaps of the slain, and blood enough to tinge with deep red the largest rivers. It was anger that overturned those most noble cities whose foundations are now scarcely perceptible and that put to the sword the inhabitants of extensive territories, now pathless and solitary deserts. It was anger that enkindled those fires which made the sky red with their midnight flames, while they consumed so many happy homes, that poisoned refreshing fountains and brought many familes to misery and desolation. In beholding all this, you would imagine you were present at the flights of wild beasts and not the assemblies of men, except that the former are gentle among themselves, whereas the latter kill one another with a mutual spirit of destruction.

Moreover, anger has this destructive quality, *viz.*, it effaces from man the likeness of his God, whose works are stamped with tranquillity. Anger obscures the mind so that it cannot see the truth nor attend to the advice of another; it disturbs and perverts all the faculties of the soul; and while its deadly influence affects the entire man, sinking him to the lowest level of degradation, scarcely does he incur the odium which this vice deserves, for most people are so blind in this matter that they think indeed it is all right to be angry. But if we cannot subdue this passion altogether, we had better approach those remedies by which it may be subjected to the empire of reason and restrained within sensible bounds.

The best remedy for anger is to be speedy in disdaining the first provocation to it and in extinguishing those sparks arising from it that threaten to blaze into a flame, for if once it begins to turn you out of the way of salvation, your return to that way shall be very difficult. Anger will do all that it wishes and not just that which you may permit it to do. When an enemy has marched within the gates of a city, he does not receive laws from a people who are made his captives. Wherefore, it is easier to deny evil access into your breast than to master it when once admitted.

The higher regions of the universe, which are regulated by superior laws and are near to the stars, are neither obscured by clouds nor agitated by storms, but enjoy undisturbed calm, while the lower parts of creation are the spheres wherein the tempests roar, lightning flashes and the thunderbolts roll in terrific majesty. Hence, a soul raised to God is always full of peace as it soars in a region where tranquillity reigns; it stifles within itself those evils which inflame anger, allowing but the least possible liberty to the tongue, for it knows that anger, instead of removing any evil, only makes it worse. For as birds when caught by birdlime besmear their wings in proportion as, trembling to escape, they flap them, so every outburst of anger only increases the torment of him who is angry. This passion does us more harm than the injury which excited it. The angry man thinks that another has despised him, but he who has a knowledge of himself and of his own demerits does not vindicate himself with violence because he does not feel himself despised. Revenge is an avowal of the pain which one resents. It is not the part of a great mind to return evil for evil.

As soon as you have heard the voice of the railer's tongue, you must not attend to what you hear, but to what you ought to say. The malice of another ought not to overpower you enough to deprive you of the serenity of your own mind. God, to whom all things are possible, bears patiently with so many sinners; are not you, then—who have committed greater sins than others—able to bear even with one? It is indeed ridiculous that you should not correct your own malice, which you can do, while you waste your power in striving to remove that of others, which is beyond your reach. If you be guilty of so many sins, whatsoever you suffer is nothing when compared to Hell, which you deserve. Who, then, are you whose delicate ears cannot bear to be offended? The man who does you an injury offends himself, because he sins. What then happens to you? That which has been decreed from eternity for your salvation. Hear what God says: *"For if you will forgive men their offences, your heavenly Father will forgive you also your offences."* (*Matt.* 6:14). If this thunderbolt cannot awaken you, you are not asleep, but dead. It is necessary, then, that you should forgive the offenses of another if you wish to obtain the pardon of your own.

We must remove from the mind suspicion, that most groundless cause of anger. We fancy, indeed, that a certain person in greeting us did not show sufficient courtesy, that he interrupted us as soon as we began to speak and that his countenance seemed to frown upon us. Nor are arguments and conjectures ever lacking to support our suspicion, since we are always inclined to believe what is bad. The greater part of the injury lies in the false construction given to words and actions; wherefore, it is necessary to give a purely simple narrative of things and to pass an equally benign judgment upon them.

Plead the cause of the absent with fairness before the tribunal of your own judgment. And look upon this as a vice, *viz.*, to be too ready to believe that which we are unwilling to understand and to be angry before we have fairly judged why we are so. Patience indeed is necessary to give time for the truth to appear. You should not pass judgment on any matter, however trifling, before you have heard the witnesses nor condemn your friend before you have received his evidence. It is the part of an imprudent man to give easy credence to things of common report. Many spread falsehoods in order that they may deceive others. Others deal in the same trade because they themselves have been first deceived. He who says a thing in secret can hardly be said to have spoken it. What can be more unjust, then, than to show public anger against a secret conversation? Finally, it is not expedient to see and hear everything. The man who is ignorant of what is said of him is not offended.

When you learn that anyone has spoken ill of you, question your own conscience whether you yourself have not first spoken ill of him. Then take into consideration all that you have said. If you look into your own breast, you shall feel less particular about your honor. For why should you not pardon the excess of another, since you deny yourself nothing? Why are you so severe in the punishment of lies, whereas you yourself are a perjurer? Why are you so cruel an exactor of fidelity to principle, while you yourself violate it so often? Why have you given yourself a license to speak of others, but deny that others should take the liberty of speaking of you? Remember not only what you may have suffered from the tongues of others, but also what you may have done to make your neighbor feel your censure, and you will discover in your own bosom all you condemn in another. We are all sinners. It is our duty, then, to pardon a vice so common. And though you may be innocent as to slander, still you are capable of falling into it.

"Wherefore he that thinketh himself to stand, let him take heed lest he fall." (*1 Cor.* 10:12).

Is it a strange thing that in this world an enemy should injure you, a friend offend you, a child forget itself or a servant neglect his duty? We are as accustomed to these things as to the dew in Spring and the fruit in Summer. When a person is hastening with unusual speed through the most frequented parts of a city, it necessarily happens that he should slip in one place, be detained in another and be pushed in a third place; thus too, many impediments and complaints meet us in our way through this dissipated and unsteady life.

Why are you indignant at the injury of a wicked man? He has only done his own work. But you must practice the office of a good man if you have the grace of God in your heart. Endeavor to make him just. This, however, must be done, not in the spirit of revenge, but in patience and charity; and if you cannot succeed in making him virtuous, you will at least inspire him with affection for you. Even if you can do neither, you shall render yourself more pleasing to God.

This man has detracted you and done you a serious injury. What do you say to that? You should respond, "I do not believe it. If he has said anything, he did so under an erroneous impression, and not through malice; he wished by his zeal to do me good, or certainly I have offended him first." (It is not doing you an injury to make you suffer that which you yourself had first perpetrated.) You may say, "I admit indeed my fault;

I plead guilty; it is just to yield to justice. But suppose I am attacked without cause or any fault on my part. What then? I shall imitate Christ and say with the prophet: '*I was dumb, and I opened not my mouth, because thou hast done it.*'" (Ps. 38:10). Although the words and actions of another may be evil in themselves, they are not so to you unless you make evil use of them. The nature of things varies according to the way we use them.

What is the cause of your taking offense—because it is your opinion that you have been offended? Take away this opinion, and nothing remains to hurt you. Nothing can touch the mind of man nor enter into it; it moves itself, and everything that happens to it is of the same nature as the judgment which it passes regarding itself. Nothing can hurt you but yourself. But you will say: "He who persecutes me is a wicked man." Wait a moment; another shall make him pay the punishment which he deserves for having offended you, and already he himself has paid it in consequence of his sin. "But God has given him reason; why does he not amend?" Now, you also have received reason from your Creator, and why do you not amend your impatience? Why do you not overcome evil with good? The vices of others you keep before your eyes, but your own you keep behind your back.

But come forward, whosoever you are to whom revenge is sweet; I wish that the desired opportunity of revenge were given to you with this law—at all times just—that you should begin with the greatest injury; this is the order to be observed in those injuries and the rule you ought to follow in taking revenge: Now your anger is the greatest enemy you have; it is this that has done you the greatest injury. Begin, then, to take revenge on it. You need not go abroad to look for enemies while there is a most powerful one at home in your own house. Plato, when angry with a servant, had his hand uplifted to strike, and suspending it, said, "Would I kill you if I were not angry?" He wished to correct his anger before he chastised his servant. Be assured that an angry master is more deserving of chastisement than a negligent servant. The more virtuous a man is, the more strength he has to conquer this passion.

Judges and persons who rule the people ought sometimes to show anger, even in public—however, in such a manner that it may not run before, but follow reason, and as ancillary to it. The transgressor must be corrected and chastised, but without anger. If a good man ought to be angry at every evil deed, his whole life would be spent in anger and indignation. For in what moment will he not see things worthy of reprehension? His powers would fail him if he were angry as often as there was cause for it. Being gentle and mild towards the sinner, he will cherish the same affection towards him as a physician does to a patient affected with delirium.

As you are not moved to anger by the cold and heat which are brought on by the seasons going through their regular changes, so you ought not to be angry on account of the injuries you receive from wicked men. Those patients who do not observe temperance have lost the hope of health. The man who takes no revenge on the insolent has thereby ample satisfaction. He who injures you to make you grieve shall grieve himself if you do not, seeing himself deprived of the pleasure which he hoped to enjoy in doing an outrage. So true it is that the fruit which we pretend to reap from an injury that we inflict on anyone consists in the resentment and chagrin of him who suffers it.

If you be angry at a reproach, it appears that you know and feel it; if you disdain it, nothing will follow but its being forgotten. But you will say, "It is base to be despised and not to repair injured honor." On the contrary, it is base to fear the idea of a slight, for no one fears this except the man who deserves it. The wise man does not care what evil things may be thought of him. In his estimation of things, there is nothing base but sin. "Does someone," he says, "despise me? Let him look to it. I shall take care not to say anything worthy of being despised. Does anyone hate me? Let him look to it. It is for me to be kind and gentle to all." Thus, an invincible patience overcomes and wears out the malice of wicked men, and the forgiving man imitates his God, whose patience is infinite and who returns us countless blessings for our sins. It belongs to true courage, then, not to resent an injury, but to forgive it.

Chapter VIII

ENVY AND SLOTH

On Envy and Sloth: The description and cure of both.

ENVY PUNISHES itself before it ravages the goods of another. The other vices are pursued by the pains that punish them, but the pains of envy are accustomed to run before it, preying upon its very bowels. The envious man makes the happiness of another the cause of his own misery, and the mere sight of his neighbor's happy appearance makes him pine away. In the same hour in which this pestilence invades a man, he sins and meets his punishment. The other vices are opposed to some particular good, but envy is the enemy of all good and the perverter of the nature of things.

It is in direct opposition to the divine goodness, whose property it is to communicate all its goods—to the state of the blessed who enjoy the happiness of others as if it were their own, to Christian charity that rejoices in the prosperity even of an enemy, to the law of nature, in short, which orders us to wish others all the goods that we ourselves possess. As the eye, when affected with the disease which doctors call *Ophthalmia,* cannot see without pain anything wearing a shining appearance, so the sight of the envious man is tormented by the virtue and brilliancy of others. This vice is called envy because it sees in malignant exaggeration the excellence of another.

Satan indeed has been guilty of envy, not of the companions of his sins and punishments, but of man. But you, a man yourself, you envy your fellowmen—a sin of which even the devil himself was not guilty. This vice belongs to a little mind, which by its own judgment sinks to the level of things the most base, for you would not envy another unless you judged him to be superior to yourself. Do you wish to be free from envy? Despise the fleeting things of this world and love those of eternity. The love of eternity is the death of envy. The man who desires only eternal goods cannot envy others those which are perishable. What prince has ever envied the shoemaker or mender of old clothes their mean pursuits? A mind elevated to sublime things does not let itself down to these low objects of earth. Is it not enough that you should be tortured by your own misfortunes, which are so many in number, without the goods of others tormenting you also? Never shall you be happy if one happier is to be the cause of pain to you. Do you really think that the good things of your neighbor, which you envy, might, if taken from him, be given to you? Your neighbor has riches, is learned in the sciences and is supereminent in dignity; all these things shall be yours, if you love him. He who loves his neighbor's prosperity abounds in great riches.

I here join sloth to envy because they both are inseparable from sadness. The envious man is sad concerning the good of another; the slothful man is sad regarding his own good. Both one and the other are remarkable for littleness of mind, for *"envy slayeth the little one."* (*Job* 5:2). And sloth, which is the vice of a languishing mind, laboring under a loathing of spiritual goods and terrifying itself with the seeming magnitude and difficulty of any proposed matter, never undertakes anything worthy of a man. *"The sluggard willeth and willeth not"* (*Prov.* 13:4), always wavering and inconstant, a burden to himself and a torment to others, and by the continued irksomeness of this vice, he remains brooding over his own punishment. The slothful man is like a top, which is indeed agitated by turning round in its orb, but which does not progress beyond this, standing still by the force of the turning.

You shall find that sloth has some pretensions to resolution, but none to action. Every operation of sloth is insipid, and like lukewarm water, provokes to vomit. Such it is, not only in the eyes of men, but of God. In vain then do you hope for salvation, unless having shaken off this torpor, you make energetic resolutions and urge yourself to execute deeds of virtue by the most powerful motives. As the bird is destined to fly, so is man born to labor. The world gives each of us pain enough to induce us to give up our enterprising labors in it for the glory of God. How much does he labor who strives to gain riches? How much does that man suffer who strives to attain a long-wished for dignity? Great vices are honored and respected. But if you buy transitory goods by so much sweat, why do you not show equal diligence in securing to yourself a happy eternity? Ah, you ought to be ashamed to be so dull in a matter of such great moment! The labor indeed is short, the recompense eternal. There is nothing so arduous, nothing so difficult which the human soul, through the aid of divine grace, may not overcome. Show courage, and the specters of difficulty will soon disappear. Whatsoever the mind enjoins on itself, that it does. Do your utmost, and all things shall be possible. God helps him who is active in virtue.

Chapter IX

PRIDE, AMBITION AND VAINGLORY

On Pride, Ambition and Vainglory: An image
of the proud man. The vanity and dangers of
dignities. The evils and remedies of pride.

PRIDE, ambition and vainglory are vices that
are united to one another by a fearful alliance, from which, like the rivers of the ocean,
all evils flow. For when man proposes to himself
his own excellence as the end of his toils, he
makes all his thoughts, words and actions tend
to this alone, despising the service of God and
neglecting the respect due to his neighbor. He
fears not to tread that path which leads through
dark crimes, when it alone can conduct him to
glory. Moreover, deceits and frauds and the
destruction and slaughter of his neighbor can
raise no barriers between him and pretended
honors.

The proud man is hateful in the sight of God,
intolerable to the human race and a slave to those
base dealings by which he strives to catch the
empty praises of men. He thinks that he is entitled to a more elevated rank than the one he
enjoys, and this, like some sunny hill in the distance, he makes the dear object of his desires.

Urged on by a spirit of rashness, he dares to undertake things far beyond his reach. Of his own accord he runs himself into affairs of every sort, and extolling himself with an air of impertinence, he looks down upon others. With much art he feigns humility, that he may appear remote from the suspicion of ambition; and should he fall from his exalted state, he fills the world with his complaints, exciting quarrels and troubles around him. To his inferiors he is fierce and cruel; to his superiors he is a flatterer more timid and complying than a slave. If he possesses goods, he does not give the glory of them to God, to whom it is justly due, but arrogates it to himself. Things the most sublime, and of which he is ignorant, he speaks of in fine-spun terms, as if he knew them from his own experience, affecting to be conspicuous in everything. His curiosity respecting the actions of others knows no bounds, and while he judges them rashly, he condemns them with severity. At the same time that he magnifies their vices, he diminishes their praises. In his words and carriage you can see nothing but arrogance and contempt for others; he hates correction, slights good counsel and disdains to follow the friendly advice given him; he fancies that he has goods which indeed he lacks, and his notion of those which he has far surpasses the reality. The worst crimes will not stop him if he should not be preferred before all others and if he suspects that he and what belongs to him are slighted. His heart resembles the sea in a storm, it being continually agitated by violent emotions; he becomes the sport of a thousand anxieties, because the honor which he desires depends upon another. *"Pride is the beginning of all sin."* (*Ecclesiasticus* 10:15).

If you be wise, weigh as on a scale the least particle of eternal happiness and compare it with whatsoever seems to you most desirable in this life—kingdoms, empires, in short, the whole globe; without a doubt, this particle of the glory of Heaven will outweigh the whole universe, with all its pomps, and sweep them before it as the wind does the leaf in Autumn. Raise your heart, therefore, to those eternal goods and render yourself worthy of Heaven, for which you were created. Banish all proud thoughts of your own excellence and strive to measure your strength with those true goods that shall never fail. If Caesar had adopted you for his son, who could bear your haughty looks? But you are at present the son of God, redeemed by the Precious Blood of Christ. Why do you not reflect on your noble origin? Why do you lower yourself to these earthly things, altogether unworthy of your high birth? Your Father calls you to the dominion of Heaven and of the stars, to a possession that knows no end. It is for this then that you ought to conceive the most sublime hopes, pouring forth acts of glory and praise and exulting in the high nobility which you have received from the Father, and to regulate your moral conduct according to the example which He has given you. This is the path which leads to true glory.

When called to the divine tribunal, what shall be your views concerning scepters and crowns in this world? They shall appear as but brilliant fetters and splendid miseries; and if the scales were fallen from the eyes of men to allow them to see the truth, they would not enter into so many furious contests to ascend to the throne. There are more would-be kings than kingdoms. A great worldly fortune is great slavery. Those whom the world pronounces happy are not so in their own minds, for the happiness in which they seem to rejoice is only a dead weight upon themselves, while it makes them an insupportable burden on the people under them. Under pressure from the cares of this world they indeed praise a life free from trouble and spent in sweet tranquillity. Then they entertain the darkest hatred for that splendor which before they so much admired; then, astonished and trembling, they speak in terms of solid wisdom of the vanity of earthly things; then they dread death and the judgments of God, in whose presence that dignity—which was sought by so much anxiety, procured by so much sweat and purchased oftentimes even by blood—is of no avail. But you should live in such a manner, however, that you may appear with confidence before the tribunal of the Divine Justice. For he who humbles himself now shall be exalted hereafter.

You are foolish if you suppose that the dignity which you have acquired (supposing that you are

elevated to the throne) can render you secure
and tranquil. What was once lawful for you shall
be so no longer. In lofty positions the liberty for
committing faults is less; for the higher you are
raised, the more notorious your vices shall
become to all around you. He who stands on the
top of a house cannot conceal himself there. If
in times past you enjoyed any repose, it is now
perished. It is no longer allowed you to remain
in private life, nor can you spend one day as you
would wish. The falls from high situations indeed
are great. In vain do you seek for repose in a
place where all have found danger and labor,
and many even a miserable end. Royal tables do
not sustain sumptuous banquets without some
peril; poisonous concoctions are drunk in cups
of gold ornamented with gems. How many kings
have purpled the throne with their own blood?
High places are slippery, and all things there seem
suspended in the air and threatening to fall. It
is safer to walk along the plain, for the number
of those who envy you is not less than the multitude engaged in admiring and applauding you.
How many are laying snares for you in private
or attacking you openly? You can place no reli-
ance on your servants, your friends, your son,
your brother. But the humble and retired dwell-
ing alone is happily removed from those crimes,
and the man who lives unknown to the world
enjoys security. He fears no one whom no one
fears.

If you should see a horse or a dog assuming

superiority over the rest of the animals of the same species, how could you refrain from laughter? But you yourself are more deserving of laughter if you extol yourself above others because indeed you may be richer or more powerful than they happen to be. *"Why is earth and ashes proud?"* (*Ecclesiasticus* 10:9). A person cannot glory except in his own proper good. But what good have you that you have not received from God? Sin is the only thing that you can call your own. If then you have received all manner of good things from God, to Him alone give the glory thereof. Do we prefer one horse to another on the grounds that it has much fodder and barley and is decorated with a golden bridle and a saddle enriched with gems? By no means, for the one that is swifter in the race wins the prize.

Thus man, unless indeed he be the child of folly, should not seek glory from anything which is outside himself. But you will say, "I am better and more noble than others." Now this very fancy renders you unworthy of all honor, because no one is worthy of honor but the good man who disdains honor and glory. True nobility knows not what it is to be extolled, and where unaffected modesty is found, there honorable life loves to dwell. The greatest glory of the great is to humble themselves as much as possible.

Reflect on the fragile elements of which your nature is composed, and with a rule, measure the dimensions of your little body. In this you shall find much to humble yourself and nothing to make you proud. Despise not the system of geometricians and philosophers who teach that the whole earth is but a point. Oh, how miserably foolish are you to establish kingdoms and divide realms in this "point"? In a narrow compass no person is great. This earth, which you proudly trample underfoot, will quickly embrace you in its bosom, nor shall you possess one inch more of it than that which your cold and putrid remains shall occupy. Go now, and in this nothingness build great and immortal edifices. Here give full vent to your unbridled passions and exercise your swelling insolence. Here allow your base desires full scope for gratification; here levy armies and fight battles. When you shall have displayed much madness, you shall know, when it is too late, how vain are the titles of honor and how false the dignities of the world. Everything here that glitters is like glass which shines when it is broken. Large trees take many years to grow, but in one hour they are torn up by the roots.

You shall cut off a powerful motive to pride if you retire into private life. No one seeks to be magnificent in his own eyes nor in those of a small circle of his domestics and friends, but the proud man courts the presence of all the people in order to display the magnificence of his pride and vanity. Who clothes himself in rich purple to exhibit himself in secret? Who seeks a solitary place in which to prepare a banquet on

plates of gold? Who displays the pomp of his luxury while retired alone under the shade of a rus-
tic tree? Ambition seeks eagerly for the public
stage, nor does it exert itself anywhere more
powerfully than amid the plaudits of men. If the
bee makes honey, the horse runs, the tree bears
fruit, they seek nothing more. But man desires
applause and to be pointed out with the finger,
while it is said of him, "This is the man." But
if you consider attentively the character of those
persons by whom you wish to be praised, there
is nothing you will more easily disdain than the
applause of the popular crowd; they are vain and
inconstant men whom you oftentimes pronounce
foolish, who condemn themselves at every hour
of their own foolishness and who often reject
their own advice.

Life is short both for him who praises and for
him who is praised; and it is spent too in a cor-
ner of the earth, which is only a mere point;
nor do all agree in this praise—excepting him who
is praised. But, it may be urged, "It is something
grand to be praised by posterity, by those whom
you have never seen nor ever shall see." Why
do you not grieve that you have not been praised
by those who lived long before your time? But
suppose that those who are mindful of you were
immortal and that their memory of you should
never die: what would this profit you when you
are dead? What does it profit you now while you
are living? You are often praised for what good
you do not possess and criticized despite the fact

that you *do* possess some good quality. The real value of anything is found within itself, nor is it better in itself for having been either praised or not praised. Does the sun lose any of its light if its spectators absent themselves from it? Does the fig lose its sweetness, the flower its beauty, the gem its brightness, unless they be celebrated with praises and encomiums? It is a mark of illustrious birth when a person disdains the praises of men and is content with himself. When you desire praises, you are unworthy of them, for what is praiseworthy in you? How great is your weakness, how great your misery and how awful the uncertainty of your salvation! Although you may have done all that duty demanded of you, still you are *an unprofitable servant.* (Cf. *Luke* 17:10). But with what face can you dare assert that you have fulfilled your duty in everything? Tremble lest you be not as good as people believe you to be, and beware lest they praise those things in you with which you yourself are displeased. Give to God all you have received from Him: your being, your life and your understanding. Nothing remains but your sin. Therefore, since you are nothing, your glory must be in nothing. When you shall understand that you are nothing, *then* indeed you shall begin to be something.

Chapter X

CONTROL OF THE BODY AND EXTERNAL SENSES

On Control of the Body and the External Senses: How far the body is to be indulged. The liberty of the eyes is to be restrained. Extravagance of dress is to be condemned.

FOLLOW this sound and beneficial rule of life: to give no more to the body than what is good for its health. We must use a strong hand against it, lest it refuse to obey the mind. It is indeed necessary to indulge it, but not to become its slave. We must attend to its various needs arising from hunger, thirst, nakedness and a houseless state, all of which must be supplied. But as to the rest, which luxury demands for ornaments, stand in fear and trembling at the mere sight of them, for by these, snares are prepared for the soul. The man who loves his body too much and entertains excessive fears for it despises all its moderate provision. You are too noble and are born for things too sublime to become the slave of your body, which you cannot consider but as the prison and chains that deprive your soul of its liberty. A wise and virtuous man takes care of his body, not because he should live for it, but because he cannot live without it. The body is only the instrument of the soul. What artist, to the utter neglect of his art, loses all his time in the arrangement of his instruments? Truly, the man who makes his body the great concern of his whole life lives as if he had no spirit.

Whereas the senses are the windows of the soul by which spiritual death often enters upon it, endeavor to transfer the service of the senses from an earthly to a celestial life, and lead them sweetly from that excessive application to the business which engages them, lest they too greedily plunge themselves, and your soul, into the delights of perishable things. It is the duty of the senses to obey and not to command.

Before all things, it is necessary to restrain the liberty of the eyes, for truly their glances are as swift as thought and carry the images of many things to the imagination and thence to the understanding, awakening at the same time the seeds of sin in concupiscence—unless a close guard be placed on them. But when the purity of the interior eye accompanies the rectitude of that of the exterior, you shall discover the traces and footsteps of the Divinity in everything; and when you shall have learned to respect God in His creatures, your mind shall from these things soar on angelic wings to the contemplation of the Divine Majesty Itself.

A woman gaudily dressed is the finished image of impurity. Never fix your eyes upon her, for

if you do, you shall perish. You ought not to be
a spectator at comedies, dances or theatrical
plays, for they dissipate the mind and engage
it in those delusive ideas that prevent it from
rising to Heaven. Where the eye errs, there the
affections also err.

The hearing is the sense related to knowledge.
It is the door by which the knowledge of truth
and wisdom enters the spirit. Let prudence then
guard the entrance to your ears, lest falsehood,
instead of truth, and folly, instead of wisdom,
rush into the secret recess of your heart. Shut
your ears against slander and whispering trifles;
shut them against idle tales and everything which
does not conduce to the welfare of the soul. As
he who has heard pleasant music carries away
the melody in his ears, so an evil discourse,
although it may not act immediately, deposits
its seeds in the mind, which long remain there
and from time to time present themselves to the
mind. The more seldom we hear men outside ourselves, the more frequently shall we hear God
speaking within ourselves.

The perfumes that have been invented with
so much art ultimately represent the fruitless
efforts of men who have given themselves up
to fostering an effeminate and oftentimes bad
life. Wherefore, having removed all those perfumes far from you, make for yourself an odor
of sweetness by the practice of moral virtues.
Thus you will chastise the taste by abstinence
and sobriety, and the touch you will mortify with

haircloth and discipline, a harder bed and other austerities. It is better to preserve the body by chastising it than to destroy it *and* the soul entirely by harmful indulgence.

Since the disposition and ornament of the body make known the interior state of the soul, you should remain far from those things which are the signs of a depraved and disorderly mind. The pagan sages of old did not permit their disciples to move the tip of a finger without a reason for it. A rectitude so rigid I would not require of you, but I wish this and proclaim it: that you abstain from immoderate laughter, vulgarity and the sinful liberty of the corrupted—in short, from affected gestures and an unbecoming walk. In order that nothing may appear in you which can wound the eyes of your beholders, let there be nothing remarkable in the way of perfumes on your garments, in the severity of your countenance, in the irregular movements of your body or in any marks of contempt for others. One can do many things honestly by himself which cannot, without wounding modesty, be done in the presence of others.

Man was created in a state of nakedness and was not ashamed, for he could not blush at a nudity of which he was not conscious. But afterwards he sinned, and having thrown away the robe of innocence which had been once sufficient to cover him, he found it necessary to use external garments to hide his shame. But what was at first a badge of our fallen state has now become a mark of dignity. Garments are now sought, not only for covering, but for ornament, which pleases the eyes of men and accords with their passions.

The garments that we wear are the index of our minds. An excessive nicety in dress and of the whole appearance of one who stands at once before the mirror and the casket, shows forth an effeminate mind. You would feel ashamed of external ornaments if you only thought of what they cover. The man who enjoys the interior ornaments of virtue does not seek those that are external. Virtue loves to appear without paint, and whatsoever you add to it is less than itself. To glitter in purple robes and leave the mind in filth is an error full of human vanity. Some load themselves with chains, but because these are made of gold, they do not fear the infamy of slavery. Others do not bind, but rather pierce themselves with gold, for they fix it in their wounded ears, from which oftentimes a keepsake hangs, and therefore, what was formerly a punishment in having to clothe ourselves is now our ambition. You shall see not a few occupied a long time between the comb and the mirror, more anxious to decorate their head than to save their souls.

Thus the corrupt judgment of foolish men has prevailed over their minds, so that they ornament themselves with things which they ought to trample underfoot. Therefore, do not wear gaudy clothing; let your clothing be made not for show, but for necessity (below what is stately and above what is shabby) and suited to your state of life. Even if you were decked out in gold and pearls, without the beauty of Christ, you would be deformed. This is that beauty which never dies and that ornaments not mortal flesh but the immortal spirit. It is ambitious foolishness to cover filthiness with gold.

Chapter XI

CARE OF THE TONGUE

On the Care of the Tongue: Its importance and difficulty. What is to be observed and avoided in conversation. How we are to bear the evil tongues of others.

IT IS A matter of as great importance to guard the tongue as it is the pupil of the eye, because *"Death and life are in the power of the tongue."* (*Prov.* 18:21). He who cannot govern his tongue is like a city without walls, which is exposed on all sides. Without the grace of God, however, it is next to an impossibility to tame it. Man tames the lion, the bull and the bear, but his tongue he cannot tame. Human nature loves to talk much, as it rejoices to give immediate expression to its desires and conceptions. Moreover, the tongue is fixed near the brain, as the mouth is near the faculty of thought, in order that whatsoever the mind thinks may be quickly conveyed to the organ of speech and published in words. Nature itself has taught you how necessary it is to guard the tongue, since it has placed a double barrier (in the teeth and the lips) before this member. But as the fragrance of the sweet ointment evaporates if the box in which it is kept be left open, so all the vigor of the mind is dissipated when the mouth is not closed. That man forgets himself who is not always mindful of guarding his tongue.

Be prudent in every conversation, suppressing that immoderate inclination which rashly hurries most people on to pass sentence upon their neighbor without due examination and deference to the case in question. Flee far from duplicity and deception, and without any ambiguity or equivocation deliver the pure sentiments of your mind. God has given you the faculty of speech that you may truly and candidly announce things as they really are. Before you speak, consult your conscience—as to whether you be influenced by any evil passion—nor should you permit your tongue to say a word until that influence cease; otherwise, you shall say many things of which you shall afterwards have to repent. You may easily keep silence if you allow no passion to disturb your heart and if you preserve your soul tranquil and serene. Your discourse and your mind ought to be stamped with the same character. If your mind be sound, temperate and composed, your discourse also will be prudent and temperate. If the former be corrupted, the latter will breathe corruption. It is language that reveals to us the character of him who speaks.

Your conversation ought not to be of an idle nature. You ought to be as particular in the choice of your words as you are in that of your food. You examine the bread that you eat; why not do the same with the words you speak, which have often raised greater disturbances in your house than your food has caused in your stomach. Accustom yourself to speak much with yourself and little with others. Wise men have often regretted having spoken, but never having kept silence. Those animals are esteemed more sagacious whose voice is least heard. Talkativeness is the vice of children, and of women in whom reason is not strong. Any man who speaks nothing but vain and useless words has no virtue. If you love God and your salvation, your discourse will be on God, virtue and perfection. Charity is a stranger to falsehood, nor can it disguise itself. Everyone is immersed in the things which he loves, and these form the subject of his conversation. Hence you speak less willingly of divine things because you have not as yet arisen from the dross of your vices. I must add, you ought to read and meditate a little, at least on subjects regarding your salvation. How could matter on this fail you if you wish to speak to yourself? *"For out of the abundance of the heart the mouth speaketh."* (*Matt.* 12:34).

Almost every discourse among men turns on the life, morals and pursuits of others; and there are almost as many judges passing sentence upon each one as there are inhabitants in his city. Scarcely does anyone look at home. We are for the most part near-sighted with regard to our own faults, but in discerning those of others, our vision is very good. We throw wide open our doors to receive reproaches against our neighbor, but hardly do we leave a chink open to hear anything in his praise. It behooves us, in places where this vice is more common, to be more careful in avoiding it. You have plenty to do with your own vices—find fault with these and correct them. Do not divulge your own secrets, or those of others which you are obliged to conceal.

Many have fallen into great disputes because they revealed their secrets to imprudent persons to whom they ought not to have confided them. Usually, to tell a thing to one person is the same as telling it to many. A word easily flies from one to another, and from these to all. This arises from the extent of discourse, to which many people fix no just bounds. The pleasure which one feels in conversation insensibly draws him on, and like drunkenness, so occupies the mind that there is no secret so hidden and sacred which may not travel abroad and become public. A man reveals to you his secrets; you in return, having received a pledge of confidence, communicate yours to him. But you perhaps may keep these secrets, while he tells everyone he meets the secret things he has heard, so that everyone knows, under cover of a secret, that of which all were ignorant in public.

You may well say that tongues take wings to fly privately to the ears of all, until the secret extends far on all sides and becomes a report. Whatsoever evil is under Heaven generally owes its origin or advancement to the tongue; therefore, make a balance for your words and a bridle for your mouth. You ought to say nothing of which it would be better to keep a profound silence. Stinginess in words is more praiseworthy than that in money. The man who scatters his money benefits others, while he injures himself; he who lavishes his words injures both himself and others. The person who knows how to hear much and say little approaches near to the Divinity.

Nothing can be secure from the darts of the tongue: It is not arrested by the power of kings nor by the virtue of saints; the one needs not dread the sword, and the other cannot fear censure, yet neither can hide from calumny. Christ Himself, when living among men, did not escape the scourge of the tongue. Imitate Jesus and the Saints in their example of patience. Detraction is both a spur to urge men to the practice of virtue, and a bridle to hold them in the right way.

There is no enemy among the vices more powerful than censure. When anyone speaks ill of you, he teaches you what you ought to avoid. Do you wish to escape the darts of the envenomed tongue? Disdain them. If you observe silence, you shall receive no wound. Esteeming much the judgment of the good, you need not fear the insolence of the calumniator. It concerns you but little what others may think of you; in your own conscience you have a more certain and incorruptible witness. Interrogate your conscience and believe it.

What can be more unworthy of you than to rest your character on the saying of the unwise and to submit it to the judgment of another? It is necessary that you should be good, let others say what they will of you, as if gold or emerald should say, "Whatsoever they may think, it behooves me to be what I am by nature and to preserve my color." If anyone should say injurious words to the limpid fountain, shall it therefore cease to pour out pure water? And if a person should throw dirt into it, does it not presently clear itself, dissipating the filthy matter?

Thus, neither ought you to disturb the calmness of your mind, although the wicked should calumniate and tear you to pieces. To be disturbed at every rumor is to have but little regard for oneself. Children strike with their little hands the mouth of their father; the infant pulls the hair of its mother, gnawing her bosom, tearing her cheeks and spitting on them, and we call none of these things an injury, because he who does them is incapable of conceiving such an act. Do you also entertain the same sentiments for those who calumniate you as parents cherish for their children? If once you let yourself be moved by anger on account of an injury, becoming weak-minded thereby, you honor him who is the cause of it. It is necessary, then, that you should have the glory of being admired by him from whom you could bear to suffer disdain. But this is the vice of a base soul and a little mind. You shall always be unhappy if you imagine yourself despised.

Chapter XII

THE INTERIOR SENSES

*On the Interior Senses: The usage of opinions;
the mind must be imbued with good thoughts.
Concupiscence and its depraved affections are to
be restrained. Various injunctions to this effect.*

THE GREAT hinge upon which wisdom turns
is that no opinion should cling to the mind
which does not accord with nature and reason.
Wherefore, rejecting all other opinions, you ought
to fight against the sallies of the imagination as
logicians do against the false reasoning of
sophists. A son is dead; this is no evil, as we
cannot preserve life. His father disinherits him;
and this too is no evil, since we can have no
control over it. But if the father grieves exces-
sively on this account, his grief being within the
province of his will, it is an evil. He receives
this disgrace with fortitude, and this also—
depending on the will—is a blessing.

If you accustom yourself to this practice, you
shall advance in virtue. Your friend is cast into
prison? What happens? Nothing, except his
imprisonment. But everyone who adds anything
of his own perverse opinion to an event may
indeed say that a misfortune has befallen him.

Rectify your opinion, and all things shall be tranquil. As we bind the madman lest he hurt anyone, so we must restrain the imagination, lest it overwhelm the mind with a multitude of false opinions. The imagination, like a wild beast, gets away and through excess of liberty wanders at large wheresoever it pleases, babbling, hurried, restless, fond of novelty and ignorant of moderation. To this understanding apply yourself diligently, that you may hold and bind as in one place this inclination, lest your thoughts resolve and rest upon mere fancy. In truth, you are in no way concerned with anything that is outside your mind.

Examine diligently everything that presents itself to your thoughts, in order that you may be able by the force of reason to see its nature as distinct from everything else, as also its properties, circumstances and utility. Consider whether it concerns you and whether it be in your power or not. If it does not concern you, do not give it any access into your mind, and fight against it as much as you can. God, being intimately present to all things, sees most clearly the hidden recess of your heart, and nothing is so secret that it is not open to His eyes. Be careful, then, lest you think of anything of which you would blush to speak before an honest man. Let your thoughts be placid, simple, pure and without any malice—so holy that, if you were suddenly asked what your thoughts were, you might be able without shame to make public what passed in your interior. It would be a disgrace to think on anything of which it would be a dishonor to speak. You ought to shut the door against evil thoughts if you desire to be always engaged in those that are good.

Nothing is more harmful to the soul than concupiscence, that is our passions or emotions, which like the brute seeks only things of the senses. This is the source of most sins and imperfections; this is the enemy that you ought always to fear and oppose until made subject to reason—as much, at least, as this frail life will permit. Here the war is perpetual, without rest or truce. We must fight without any regular line of battle until our dying day, because the enemy is as disorderly as he is incessant in his attacks upon us. He lies lurking within you; nay, you yourself are your own enemy, and more powerful than the army of Xerxes.

Preserve your soul from yourself. It is a more difficult thing to subject yourself than to take cities, and to remain master of yourself than of the whole universe. I do not insist that you should beat down and quite annihilate your passions, but that you learn to govern them. Your reason has done enough in having restrained and moderated them. The stoics were in error saying that all our affections were evil. The household of nature is neither evil nor vain. He who takes away all the affections takes away all virtue. Where there is no battle, there is no victory.

This struggle is indeed as dangerous as the outcome is doubtful, for the passions are born with us, and reason comes only some years afterwards, when they have already established their empire; and the will, deceived by a vain appearance of good, obeys them without resistance, until reason, having in the progress of time and by the force of experience ascertained its powers, gives notice of its right to command the passions and oppose their tyranny. You cannot indeed correct the first motions of nature, but you ought to watch over yourself with great vigilance, and when you see that you are disturbed, then restrain, as if by a bridle, the unruly emotion. It is easier to resist the beginning than to control the progress of the passions.

If you foresee all possible casualties before they take place, so that the enemy may find you prepared for him, you shall in a short time arrive at great peace of mind. After the danger, it is too late to receive instruction. Learn, then, to do and to say few things, for if you remove that which is not necessary from all you do and say, you shall have fewer troubles of mind. Nor should you say that this matter is small, it is of no importance. The commencement of virtue and perfection may indeed appear very small, but nevertheless, it is something most grand.

The "old man" within us, whose origin is derived from the infected seed of fallen Adam, may be contemplated as a certain tree whose roots are self-love, having propensity to evil for its trunk, turbulent passions for its branches, bad habits for its leaves, and thoughts and words and deeds which are opposed to the Divine Law for its fruit. Lay the axe to the root, therefore, and cut down the tree of your most wicked self-love, lest the branches of depraved affection shoot forth into leaves and fruit. If you manfully cut down this tree, you shall, as if by one blow, lay flat the whole evil offspring of concupiscence. Now you shall cut it down and eradicate it if you despise yourself and truly believe that you alone out of thousands are not gifted by any special favor and that you are destitute of any knowledge or virtue, if you do not fear to displease men, or to be despised by them, and if you do not fear willingly to be destitute of every solace and comfort. You shall preserve yourself if you cherish a salutary hatred for yourself, but you shall be your own destruction if you love yourself with irregular affection.

Chapter XIII

LOVE

On Love: Its nature, causes and effects; its remedies. Some remarks on hatred.

LOVE IS the complacency we feel in good. It is the first impression by which the appetite is affected by some known good, that common chain which links together the whole universe; and it is the first of the affections, by having vanquished which, you easily overcome the rest. Divine love tends to the origin from which it first arose; it inclines to good because it came from the Sovereign Good. Examine your life and place your heart on the scale of severe investigation to see what kind of love prevails in it, for that object which preponderates in the scale of love is your God—or rather the ''idol'' which you adore. Wherefore, God commands you to love Him with your whole heart, wishing to possess the first of your affections, because the object you love with your whole heart, this you adore as your God.

It is not only goodness and beauty that engage our love, but certain fellow-feelings and like-nesses of minds and manners. Likewise, exterior modesty, industry, nobility, learning, genius and

the other advantages of mind and body are so
many causes to excite love. Indeed, love itself
is a lodestone to attract love, and if you join
benefits to love, he who was first unwilling to
love will, from a mutual feeling, be forced to
return love for love. There are, moreover, certain things that naturally excite us to love, for
those whose spirits are lighter, hearts warmer,
blood more subtle and whose manners are of a
sweeter temperament than others are more
inclined to love.

Great is the power of love; it transforms him
who loves into the object loved. Love is a kind
of ecstasy, a certain journey from oneself, a species of voluntary death. Every lover is absent
from himself, thinking nothing, providing nothing and doing nothing for himself, and unless
he be found in company with the object of his
love, he is nowhere.

Oh, how unhappily does he love who loves not
God! For that man who loves earthly things—
which cannot satisfy the soul because they are
finite and subject to vanity and death—cannot
find his being in the object of his love. But he
who loves God is in Him and, ceasing to live in
himself, lives in God, in whom all things live and
where is our center and Unchangeable Good.
Human love is vehement and bitter; divine love
is always humble, always tranquil. Jealousy torments human love, but the divine love has no
rival. The one fears lest another may love; the
other wishes all to love. Wherefore, if you love

yourself, love God, for it is to you and not to Him that this love is beneficial. Man is subject to change and to death; God you never lose, unless He has lost you.

In order that your love for your neighbor may be pure, you must remove from it all human motives arising from inclination, pleasure and likeness and seek to found it only on those which agree with piety and sanctity. That love which they call Platonic is the ruin and death of virtue, because it supposes that the soul, from the view of earthly beauty, is raised to the contemplation of the beauty of God. Rather, the steadfast looking at a beautiful face creates the desire of touching it, and that which goes out through the eyes, whether it be light or cupidity, enervates and destroys man. It is less dangerous for your feet to err than your eyes.

But the remedies for love are most difficult, for when it is corrected, it becomes most violent, and unless you oppose its beginning, it steals by degrees upon you, so that you are in love before you have resolved to love. But if you altogether resist its first approach, the cure is easy. Let the mind also be engaged in other things that require care, and call the thoughts away from love. After all this, it is necessary to flee from that which made you think on the beauty of the object of your love, for there is nothing more easily renewed than love, which if once it take hold of you, will torment you with so much obstinacy that it cannot be removed, until exhausted, it dies in the slow course of time.

Shame has cured many when they had the mortifying grief to see themselves pointed at and become the laughingstock of people and have considered that this passion is full of baseness and danger and a subject for repentance. Others have reaped much fruit in attentive reflection on the evils and inconveniences which hang over the beauty and attraction of the loved object. Finally, this consideration will assist you much to turn your love to God, to virtue and to eternal rewards—to those things which are truly worthy of your love—so that divine love will banish the love of earth, and the generous mind of man will make him blush to be defiled by earthly affection. Evil affections corrupt good morals.

Love is that golden bond by which nature binds all things together. It is this that assembles the choirs of the stars in the heavens, the flocks of birds in the air, the herds of oxen in the pastures, the sheep congregated on the mountains and the wild beasts in the forests. But hatred alone destroys this sacred union, for as love tends to union, so hatred inclines to division and dissension. This is the passion into which ignorant, timid and suspicious persons easily fall, fearing loss on all sides. There are some persons whose nature is such that they detest the whole world and who, like birds of ill omen, hate even their own shadows. If you meet any of these, do not hate but pity them.

As in playful wrestling you avoid anger with

your companion, so in the affairs of life shun
hatred against him who is opposed to you. Truly,
you will crush your hatred by exciting your heart
to the love of some good quality in the person
whom you hate. Hatred will find no place in you
if you interpret everything in a good sense. It
is necessary, besides, to turn your hatred against
those things which well deserve it—the deformity of sin and eternal perdition. If you turn
your hatred on other things, you do not injure
them, but yourself, for if God commands you to
love your enemies, whom ought you to hate? You
must travel beyond the universe to find one on
whom to waste your hatred. Sin alone—which
is outside the nature of things—deserves your
hatred, but if you hate any person, let that person be yourself, as all the world cannot injure
you as much as you can injure yourself.

Chapter XIV

DESIRE AND FLIGHT

*On Desire and Flight: What we ought to desire
and from what we ought to flee.*

HAPPY is the man who is subject to God and
who is not too anxious about anything, con-
forming himself to Him in all things, and who
says: "Does God wish me to be in health or in
sickness, rich or poor? Whether He wishes me
to depart from this world or to remain here, I
am prepared for both." If once you begin to say,
"When shall I go there, when shall I have that?"
you shall be miserable. For if you desire anything
outside yourself, you shall be tormented by perpetual anxiety and placed in a situation similar
to that of walking a treadmill—always going but
never advancing. Your thoughts, affections and
all your actions are in your power. You cannot
say the same of your body, riches, glory, dignity
and all else that is beyond the sphere of your
actions. Your thoughts, etc. cannot be controlled
by anyone; your body, riches, etc. are foreign to
you and subject to a thousand accidents. For this
reason, you should not desire these things at all,
or at least if you do, it should be with due moderation, knowing that they depend upon the will

of another and that they cannot remain long with you, which the nature of things imperatively demands. There is nothing external that is truly desirable, *"for the fashion of this world passeth away."* (*1 Cor.* 7:31). And even if all things accede to your wishes, still you must in death—full of grief and against your will—forsake all you possess. Look into yourself: you shall there discover a fountain of good, always gushing out, if you always dig for it.

The wisdom of the ancient philosophers was centered on this point: that, withdrawing themselves from the empire of fortune, they with happy minds disputed concerning happiness, though they were in the midst of the most cruel torments. For when they considered the bounds of that power given by the Almighty to man, they persuaded themselves that nothing but their passions and thoughts belonged to themselves, and so great was the command that they gained over themselves by this study, that they governed the motions of their minds in a manner which made them boast—and not without some reason—that they alone were rich, powerful and happy. But assiduous meditation is necessary in order that you may learn to disdain things beyond yourself as not really concerning you. If you could reach this point, you would never grieve that you lack external things, as you would not grieve that you are not king of the Tartars or that you have no wings with which to fly. All things outside of us are as nothing to us.

Behold the rein [i.e., the realization that only our thoughts and emotions truly belong to ourselves] by which our desires are to be restrained, and if you do not set bounds to them, you shall never be able to satisfy the mind, which in its own nature is insatiable, and all that you may give it will not satisfy its desires, but only augment and irritate them the more. No liquid can suffice for him whose bowels are burning with excessive heat, for that is not thirst but disease. The same happens to those who do not subject their desires to the laws of reason (which has its own bounds), but to vice and luxury, whose imperious caprice can neither be bounded nor conceived. You shall feel no inconvenience nor shall you lack anything you desire if you confine yourself within the limits which nature prescribes for you. If you exceed those, you shall be poor, even in the midst of great riches. Nothing can satisfy cupidity, but only a few things satisfy nature.

Remember that we must conduct ourselves in life as we should at a banquet. If the dishes be carried about and come to you, stretch forth your hand and modestly take a portion for yourself; if the attendant passes you by, do not stop him. If he should not as yet approach you, do not show you are hungry, but wait until he comes. If you be thus affected towards riches, dignities and other things that are outside yourself, you shall be worthy of the banquet of the Saints and shall enjoy that peace of mind which will make you superior to all the events of life. But if you disdain and reject even those things that are within your legitimate province, you shall share not only in the banquet of the Saints, but also in their happiness, and you shall begin to taste that happiness on earth which they enjoy in Heaven. You can therefore make yourself happy if you desire no external thing. Who is happy? The person who has what he wishes. But he has what he wishes who desires nothing but what he can possess.

There are many things from which we flee and that are hateful in our eyes because they seem harmful and opposed to us, but which are in fact truly useful to us, for it often happens that things which may be unpleasant to the taste are profitable to the spirit. The things that hurt us often at the same time instruct us. Death, exile, poverty, ignominy, labor, sickness and other things of this kind which are not within your power are not evil, neither should they concern you. You ought, therefore, not to avoid or detest these things, but to forget the opinion you had entertained of them. Socrates has very properly called these things masks, for as children are affrighted at masks, which have nothing in them but the appearance of horror, so it happens with you: there are many things which you are accustomed to dread, not on account of their reality, but because of their appearance. What is death? It is a mask. Behold how sweet it has been, not only to the Saints and men endowed with great virtue, but to Socrates and other sages among the pagans. What, therefore, is there horrible in death? Opinion only. The fear of death is terrible, not death itself. The same occurs in other things which you are accustomed to fear. Correct your opinion of death and of those things, and you shall find that there is nothing which you ought to dread but sin.

Chapter XV

JOY AND SADNESS

On Joy and Sadness: How a good man ought to rejoice. He who forecasts what may happen is never sad. Many remedies against grief.

YOU ought to rejoice in such a manner that modesty may appear in your joy, nor should your mind be so weakened as to hinder you from passing if necessary out of a state of joy into that of mourning. Christ Our Lord, who is the best judge of things, did not pronounce those blessed who laugh, but those who mourn. For it is very unbecoming in a Christian—who professes to seek eternal goods, who is threatened by so many dangers of soul and body and who dwells amid so many just causes of sadness—to rejoice like a fool and exult in perishable things. Earthly pleasure passes away, and those things which we call joys are often the beginning of sorrow. There is no true joy but that which arises from a good conscience, and no one but the just, the constant and the temperate can rejoice in it. In order that this gladness may ever cheer your mind, let your actions give birth to it at home with yourself. Truly this joy will be born there if its origin be within your own bosom. Other joys are vain and never fill the heart, nor do those who laugh always rejoice. True joy has an air of severity, as it arises from a good conscience, honest counsels and upright actions, from a contempt of pleasures and the calm tenor of an unspotted life. Behold the true law of virtue, *viz.*, you must mourn a long time in order to rejoice with true joy.

Sadness is an aversion over a present evil—which may be either real or apparent—accompanied by troubles and anxieties. But we are for the most part accustomed to be troubled, not by the things themselves, but by the *notion* we have of them. Do not begin an inquiry into the nature of things themselves—for instance, your land, money, business or the character of your domestics—but rather consider what your ideas of such may be. To be covered with disgrace, robbed of your money or beaten are things not in your power, but to judge of them as you ought is certainly within your reach, as well as to think that these things are not evils but things oftentimes useful. You shall be a happy stranger to grief if, turning your thoughts from present affliction, you fix them on that Blissful Home where true joys dwell. No evil ever happens to the good man—not because he does not feel it, but because he triumphs over it. He looks upon every trial as an occasion of exercising his patience, an instrument of divine grace, a path that leads to eternal glory. A good man may indeed be thought to be miserable, but he is not so in reality.

Anticipate every possible thing to happen to you

in the future. Thus you shall weaken the stroke of misfortune, which cannot take by surprise those who are prepared for it. Afflictions are insupportable only to those who think themselves secure and who keep their eyes fondly fixed on some dear object, real or imaginary. What does it matter if an unforeseen event destroys half of your property? What if it destroys all? What if your house should fall, your crops be burned and you yourself be deserted by your friends? What if you lose your reputation and be hurled from your high rank? Sickness, exile, ruin, fire and such calamities do not seem strange to the wise man. He contemplates all the future miseries that may befall him, and by meditating thus a long time, he mitigates that anguish which others can only assuage by the force of long suffering. That which happens to some may [potentially] be the fate of anyone.*

---

* "Potentially," of course, it is true that "what happens to some may happen to anyone." But there is a definite security from many "mishaps" and "accidents" if a person will live a life of solid Christian virtue, while staying in the state of Sanctifying Grace, being just to all, but especially if he will pray fervently and regularly and will practice charity and almsgiving towards his fellow man and will support Holy Church. "Charity covereth a multitude of sins," says St. Peter (*1 Ptr.* 4:8), meaning that we thereby quickly and effectively make satisfaction for our sins *on our own initiative*, and we thereby do not "force" God to teach us far more severe lessons in charity, humility and reparation by chastising us through "accidents" and "mishaps," over which, of course, He has complete control. If we will give

Ah, give me then those riches which are not followed by hunger and indigence. Show me that grandeur which knows not obscurity or extremity of contempt, that kingdom for which no ruin may be prepared. Has not this age witnessed the beheading of a queen, and that by the order of her own subjects—an example unheard of in past ages? Nor is this example far removed from those of other great personages. There is but a moment between riches and poverty, between the halls of kings and the huts of the poor, between the throne and the axe! Know then that every condition in life is subject to change and that whatsoever has befallen anyone may also befall you. The man who is always in readiness for adversity will sustain it with patience.

Virtue does not appear in a life spent in the

---

of our own free will, in advance of having things exacted from us by God, God in His turn will often bless us and keep us free from many, if not in fact all, calamities. We cannot even conceive the tender and all-consuming love God has for us; why, therefore, should He chastise us if we have already chastised ourselves in advance? However, because we cannot know for certain the state of our soul, or ever truly fathom the wisdom of God in sending trials for our correction, or for our continuance or growth in grace, we should nonetheless, as the author suggests, be prepared to face whatever misfortunes befall us, and see in them the providence of God—in either chastising us for our sins, alerting us to even greater impending danger, teaching us spiritual lessons, keeping us humble, obedient and in His grace, or increasing our merit for eternity. —*Publisher,* 1995.

sunshine of prosperity. It is only when patience calls it into action that we see what great things it can do. *"We are made a spectacle to the world, and to angels, and to men."* (*1 Cor.* 4:9). Behold a spectacle that attracts the eyes of God and which He regards as His own work. Behold a combat worthy of God—man braced in the armor of fortitude, contending against adversity and triumphing over himself and every calamity! The calm sea and the favorable wind do not call forth the skill of the pilot. *What does he know who has never been tempted?* A person says, "I am miserable because this has happened to me." On the contrary, you are blessed because you are so highly privileged as to be tested. For the same thing could have happened to anyone else, but it is not everyone who is permitted to receive such an accident without grief. You should not, therefore, succumb to adverse circumstances, but rather show fortitude in sustaining the burden placed upon you. For when you have resisted the first violent onset, you shall see that there is nothing horrible in it other than your own ideas concerning it. Natural properties are always the same and preserve themselves on all occasions. But many people patiently suffer poverty, disgrace, reproach and other things which most people esteem as misfortunes; many are insensible to them. It is not by any means natural, then, to be consumed by grief in consequence of these things, since such a reaction comes from a perverse mind. Why do you deceive yourself, therefore? By fortitude and patience you can make every calamity light. Every grief is supportable, if your own fancy does not magnify it. Take care then that your impatience does not render your burden heavier. Each person is miserable in proportion as he believes he is so.

Time wears down every malady and applies a slow but sure balm to heart-rending grief. Do you wish to know the day when your sorrow, in spite of yourself, will end? Or do you yourself want to put an end to it? Why do you not by sage counsel take that away beforehand which length of time is about to effect? After all, your grief *will* pass away, whatever care you take to preserve it. There is nothing which you get tired of sooner than grief. When it is young, it finds a consoler, and when it is old, it is laughed at. But if calamity be overcome by grief only, every day shall pass in mourning and every night in sleepless sadness; the hands shall not cease to strike the breast, and protracted grief shall exercise itself in every kind of cruelty. But tears are useless if weeping cannot assuage adversity. Learn to govern yourself and by an invincible constancy to stand up against trouble. The pilot ought to be covered with disgrace who permits the waves to carry off the rudder and who abandons the ship to the fury of the storm. He alone is worthy of praise who, while overwhelmed by the sea, holds the rudder still in his hands and contends with the swelling waves.

Chapter XVI

HOPE AND DESPAIR

On Hope and Despair: How necessary it is to restrain them.

HOPE is vain and false and indeed no more than the dream of one awaking from sleep, unless it is placed in God, who by the twinkling of His eye can make every difficulty disappear. Why do you torment yourself with the hope of something in the future and transport your thoughts so far before you? You shall hope for nothing if you wish for nothing and despise the things of the earth. No one hopes for those things which he undervalues. Although you may never have been deceived in your hopes and may have found no difficulty in realizing them, nevertheless, as they occupy so much of your time, you shall always be painfully anxious, uncertain and in doubt. As your feet do not attempt to walk in places that are impassable and steep, so your mind should not hope for things beyond your reach. This is the chief ingredient in the cup of human misery—to be frustrated in your hopes.

We must impress upon our minds that all things around us will soon perish and are at present hanging as if from a thread. Why do you forget your condition? You were born a mortal; you can promise yourself nothing, either on this day or in the hour in which you now live. Death is walking behind you. You have received what you possess from this mutual compact: that you have only the interest of all that the Sovereign Ruler has given, and at His beckoning you must again surrender up all without complaint. It is only a most wicked debtor that says injurious things to his creditor. There is nothing under the sun, therefore, which you ought to or can hope for. That hope alone is true which has the Supreme Good for its object.

Despair traces back its causes to sloth, to absence of courage, to excessive fear of difficulties, to blameworthy timidity in oneself and to loss of energy and industry. We rise above this sin by exciting the mind to exertion, after the example of others who, placed in even greater straits, nobly triumphed over their difficulties. Only begin and exert yourself—for God assists those who assist themselves—and what now seems so arduous will become most easy, if you lay aside the false notion which you had conceived regarding it. Whatsoever happens to you has been "destined" from all eternity for you. But it occurs in such a manner that you are naturally disposed to suffer it or you are not. If you are prepared for it, do not despair at all, but sustain it; if you are not disposed, still you need not despair, for whatsoever happens to you, it will soon end—at least at the close of your life.

Light indeed is everything that you can bear, and short indeed is everything that you cannot endure. But remember that you can make many things supportable, if you regard them as being useful and advantageous. It is adversity that affords an occasion of practicing virtue.

Chapter XVII

FEAR

On Fear: How vain it is and the means of over-coming it. Rashness is to be avoided. Some things again said of anger.

MANY persons, before any evil comes to their door—and indeed uncertain whether it will ever come—give themselves, nevertheless, much trouble and vexation about it. They imagine evils which do not exist and magnify those that do. The cruelty of tyrants has not invented such torments as does the mind which is too anxious about the future and that fears lest it lose present goods or that future evils befall it. By our fear we make evils which are only imaginary appear as if they really existed. What does it profit you to torment yourself by premature fears and by a vain foresight to anticipate your troubles? Is it necessary that you should be miserable before your time, because indeed you must be so some future day? It is foolish to lend yourself to reports and to be terrified by false images of evils, even the shadow of which does not exist. Often deceived by a groundless conjecture, you turn a word of doubtful meaning into a bad sense. You frequently think that the injury which you

ave done a man in power is greater than it really
s, and you do not reflect upon how much he
s angry with you, but upon how much his anger
nay injure you. But all these fears are vain, and
ecause they are so, they trouble you the more.
'or truth has its own bounds, and all that which
s uncertain ought to be attributed to the liberty
hat a timid mind takes of forming conjectures.
'he difference is small whether you suffer actual
dversity or only fear—except that your grief has
ts limits, but your fear has none. You grieve only
o the extent of the troubles which you suffer,
ut you fear for all those that are possible.

If you wish to banish every fear, consider as
aking place in the future all that which you fear,
nd measuring the magnitude of the evil, regu-
ate your fear according to it. Truly you will see
hat the evil is not great except in your own
magination. Can anything worse occur than that
xile or imprisonment shall befall you? Has the
ody to fear any punishment greater than that
f being burned or destroyed? Examine all those
hings and measure your fears against the stan-
lard of truth, and you shall find many, even
mong the pagans, who have disdained them.
t. Stephen, amid a deadly shower of stones,
almly prayed to God; St. Lawrence on the grid-
ron triumphed in the flames and rebuked the
yrant; St. Apollonia threw herself willingly on
he burning pile; Anaxarchus, while beaten with
ron mallets in the mortar, laughed; Socrates
lrank the cup of poison, rejoicing and drinking

health to Cretias. Why do you fear fire and crowd of executioners roaring like lions aroun you? Under that appearance which has terrifie the foolish hides death, which so many childre and young girls have embraced with joy. Remov the noise and tumult from these things, take awa the mask and let everything wear its own natu ral dress, and you shall see that nothing fearfu remains but timidity itself. The same thing hap pens to us of riper years as does to little chi dren. They are terrified at those whom the know, love and play with if they see ther masked. But you, worse even than children, hav arrived at so great a folly that you are tormented not only with grief but with the mask of grie and sudden fear.

You should not regard yourself in particula but the nature of man in general. Say to your self, "I have only a little body, one that is mor tal, fragile and subject to many diseases, and i the end, to death. I have made up my mind fo a long time that many miseries have been hang ing over my head. What, therefore, do I now fear Shall I be sick? The disease of the body will b the salvation of the soul. Shall I be reduced t poverty? I shall then lead a life more secure an tranquil. Shall I lose my riches? With the los of these I shall lose many cares and dangers with out end. Shall I be covered with disgrace? If justly deserve it, I shall detest the cause of it if otherwise, my conscience will console me. D I suffer from the denial of that for which I ha oped? Truly, kings themselves do not obtain all they desire. Shall I be sent into exile? I shall willingly go and turn my journey there into travels to a foreign land. Shall I become blind? The way then to many passions shall be cut off. Shall men speak ill of me? This is what I deserve and what they are in the habit of doing anyway. Shall I die? On this condition I came into this world, that I should one day leave it. But shall I die in a strange land? No land is strange to him who has '*here no lasting city.*' (*Heb.* 13:14). Shall I die before my time? No one but a madman complains that he is loosed before his time from his chains and is liberated from prison." Death, exile and mourning are not punishments to be dreaded, but debts of your mortality which are due to God. It is folly to fear what we cannot avoid.

Flee from all rashness, presuming nothing on our own powers. There is no one more quickly put down than the man who relies too much on himself. Without the help of God, from whom we receive all our strength, we make but faint efforts of our own. Rashness arises from too high an opinion of our own abilities, from contempt of our adversaries and from a hasty and inexperienced mind. The prudent man is more cautious, for he measures the extent of his own feeble efforts, examining carefully what he can do and what is beyond his power. Those who are rash, having at length found by experience greater danger in their undertakings than they

anticipated, after the first efforts, give up and
languish, too late confessing the uncertainty of
man's judgment and that all his thoughts are vain.
An imprudent feeling of security is the beginning of calamity.

Anger will never tyrannize over you if you
remove the idea that you have been injured. You
yourself open the way to sin and provoke its commission; you yourself sow the seeds of all the
misfortunes which you reap in tears. Why do you
throw the fault on others, while you throw yourself down the precipice? A man is injured by himself alone. Nurses say to children, "You shall have
it if you do not cry." With more reason you ought
to say this to your mind: "Do not be angry or
make any commotion, and what you want shall
be better done." Appoint certain days when you
determine not to be angry on any account whatsoever. Practice the same for one or two months,
and you shall find that you have so far advanced
in a little time that you shall laugh at what before
made you angry. Sweet manners are not even
so agreeable and pleasant to those with whom
one lives as to him who is endowed with them.
Behold the advantage of a peaceful mind: it lives
always in a state of joy, resembling that of
triumph.

Chapter XVIII

THE POWERS OF
THE RATIONAL SOUL

*On the Powers of the Rational Soul: The intellect
must be restrained from curiosity. The knowledge to which we must chiefly apply ourselves.
The evil of discussing the morals of others. We
must think light of the judgments of men. The
denial of the will.*

GOD HAS given us the faculty of intelligence
that we may know Him, and in knowing
Him, love Him; but sin has inflicted on our
intellect the twofold wound of ignorance and
blindness. For in your notion of truth you err, and
you are for the most part ignorant of what you
ought to do or to avoid. With what care is the city
guarded when threatened by pestilence, or the citadel fortified when besieged by a hostile army,
lest an enemy in disguise enter it. We must watch
with equal care, lest the understanding open a way
to evil through the medium of the senses. For these
present the outward forms of things which the
understanding introduces to the judgment, and
this in turn proposes them to the will. But it
belongs to the mind to admit or reject the good
or evil which the senses present to it.

The understanding must, before all things, b restrained from curiosity. Why should you l vanity distract your mind, which was created fo solid wisdom and for God? Wisdom is a thing c ineffable utility. As he who tastes poison to searc out its fatal quality shall die before he perceive its relish, so the man who pries into things whic do not concern him ruins himself before he ca know the thing for which he seeks. To kno unprofitable things is the next thing to ignoranc In order to be truly wise, one must not endeavc to acquire knowledge, but to regulate his life. person who follows this rule does not so muc seek the enjoyment as the improvement of h mind. Would you like to know the characteris tics of the stars? This knowledge is vain unles it be joined to the knowledge of your own weak ness. You wish to speak eloquently? It would b of greater advantage to you to learn to kee silence. You desire to know the news? What i newer than to renew yourself. Behold what yo ought to learn. You are delighted to confute th errors of others; why not correct your own? D you study history to know the deeds of others It is well if you be not ignorant of what you ough to do yourself. Do you feel pleasure in settlin the differences of those who are in court? Wh not harmonize your unruly passions to the dic tates of reason? If you do not seek superfluou things, you shall easily find what is necessary Truly, that knowledge alone is necessary which makes us good rather than learned.

Why do you torment and fatigue yourself with those questions which it would oftentimes be wiser to disdain than to solve? Why do you apply yourself so anxiously to the study of those things which, if you had known them, you ought to forget? We are as blameable for intemperance in study as for that in anything else. *"There is no end of making many books."* (*Ecclesiastes* 12:12). Libraries are arranged more for show than for the use of readers. It would require your whole life, though you lived many years, to read the title pages of the books that have been published. Among these books, many are injurious and dangerous; many are not worthy of being read; a good percentage are full of vanity and ignorance, which you might have read over for a long time and known nothing in the end. Some you are permitted in passing to see—only that you may disabuse your mind of their contents. But it is necessary to make a choice of a small number to read and to stop there. We do not need many books and extensive knowledge of the sciences to form our mind to virtue.

Oh, vain thoughts of mortals! We grow pale over writings and study countless arts and sciences, as if we were to live many ages; but we neglect the care of eternal life, which is not gained by the sciences, but by virtue. What does it profit you to inquire into the acts of strange kings and to describe in large volumes all that people have suffered and attempted among themselves? It would be better for you to blot out your own evils than to hand down those of others to posterity. Geometry teaches the method of measuring your estates; it would be more instructive if you learned by it to measure what would suffice for you. Arithmetic teaches you to count numbers and to make your fingers serve avarice; it ought to teach you rather to disdain and to lose with a joyful mind those things which are numbered with so much care. Music shows how to harmonize voices; let it instruct you rather, how your mind should be in accord with itself and how to make your senses conform to reason. It teaches which are the joyful and which the mournful tones; let it also teach you not to be overjoyful in prosperity nor too much cast down in adversity. I do not by any means condemn the knowledge of these things, but you may know these and other things to good purpose *after* you have known yourself and the things pertaining to your last end. Although you may know all things else, you know nothing if you be ignorant of yourself.

It is a base and shameful vice to notice the actions of others, to pry into their conduct and to interpret rashly everything they do. Who are you that you should judge another's servant? *To his own master he stands or falls.* He who will judge us all has reserved all judgment to Himself. By what audacity do you dare to invade the Divine Tribunal? Mind yourself and examine the recesses of your conscience. See the evils that exist and the good that is absent in yourself, and cease from turning your eyes upon the lives of others. You shall find an ample share of evil in yourself to censure with severity. Scarcely can we do any good which a depraved mind cannot turn to a bad sense. Heretics have abused even the Gospel; the Jews have calumniated the actions of Christ. As bodies diseased with toxicity and full of indisposition turn all they eat into bile, so an ill-disposed mind puts a bad construction on everything. A good or an evil intention often makes things good or bad, but this is known to God alone, who *"searcheth the reins and hearts. . ."* (*Apoc.* 2:23). But if your neighbor's conduct cannot be defended, what is that to you? And is it not a shame for you to make known his most hidden deformity and make a parade of it before the public? Why do you, who are worse than others, not look into yourself? Turn your reproach on yourself and speak with yourself of your own evil deeds; accuse your own depravity and judge it, for if you become your own judge, you shall avoid the judgment of God.

As we are for the most part ingenious in noting down the actions of others, in order that we may pass for persons having discernment, so we easily mistrust others for thinking or speaking ill of us, for hating and suspecting us. To overcome this vice, you must in the first place moderate that strong desire for wealth which makes you wish to please men and be esteemed by them. You must then banish the very thought of knowing what others may think or say of you, since it often happens that those whom you suspected of speaking ill of you did not so much as even think of you. Hold a soliloquy with yourself and say with the Apostle: *"If I yet pleased men, I should not be the servant of Christ."* (*Gal.* 1:10). Tell others: *"But to me it is a very small thing to be judged by you, or by man's day."* (*1 Cor.* 4:3). As you are in the eyes of God, so you are in reality! The opinion and talk of men add nothing to your goodness and diminish nothing from your malice It is infinitely better to possess the fruits of a good name than to have but the blossoms thereof.

Nothing will ever occur which shall be contrary to your own will if you deny your will altogether and transform it into the divine will. It is thus that you shall enjoy solid peace and true tranquillity of mind. You shall live as you wish—if you understand what you ought to wish for. But you ought to will that which God wills. This is the only real happiness of life—to wish that everything be done according to the will of God, and not as we wish. God leads you through mild and harsh, prosperous and adverse circumstances, to the end for which you have been destined from eternity. Submit to Divine Providence and follow it with joy, because otherwise, though you resist it, you must still follow it in spite of yourself, and by resisting it you become guilty of impiety. God conducts as if by the hand him who submits, but He forces the rebellious.

Chapter XIX

THE STATE OF THE ADVANCED

On the State of the Advanced: Various helps to aid them. The just estimation of time and the use we ought to make of it. The necessity of the presence of God.

IF YOU desire to be virtuous, first of all believe that you are sinful. Indeed, you shall never advance in virtue if you lose the desire for it. To have no wish of advancing is to go back. Continue then as you have begun and hasten quickly along the perfect way, that you may soon enjoy a mind exempt from faults and set in good order. It is an evidence of a better state of the mind if you see your vices of which you had before been ignorant. When the sick person knows his disease, we cherish a joyful hope of his recovery. Do not give too easy credit to yourself, but examine and observe yourself closely and draw proofs of your advancement from the soundness of your mind and the diminution of your passions. You shall be able to think that you are in the ranks of the advanced when you have gained great command of yourself. To possess oneself and to be always the same is a good beyond all praise. As inconstancy is the companion of vice, so uniformity of life is the characteristic of virtue.

You can, if you wish, arrive in one day at the summit of sanctity, provided your heart be turned from creatures and converted completely to God. These are the marks by which you shall know whether you live an interior life with God: *viz.*, if passing things displease you and solitude delight you; if you seek for what is most perfect; if you disdain the opinions and judgments of men. But, to make serious meditation will be a great assistance to gain every virtue. It is the book of life, in which alone, as in a rich and well-furnished library, you may find all that regards your salvation, although all other books may perish with their authors. However, it is not sufficient to know and meditate on Christ; you must imitate Him and live as if He Himself taught you by word and example. You shall never correct your irregularities unless you yourself be guided by an unerring rule.

It was well said by a certain author that those who wish to advance in virtue ought to live in such a manner as to work continually for their own improvement. For there are many things we must always keep before our minds and which throw an obstacle in the way of him who hastens up to the summit of virtue: when, for instance, you entertain an inordinate love for yourself or any creature; when you are so attached to worldly affairs that you are overwhelmed with grief if they should be lost or taken from you; when you consult too much your own sensual gratification in eating, drinking, entertainment and roving abroad; when you involve yourself too much in temporal affairs and obstinately cling to your own judgment and will; when you do not watch the motions of your heart and disdain from listening to God speaking by His secret inspirations within you. These are the principal obstacles that meet you in the path to virtue. In order to remove them, you must watch carefully and apply yourself manfully to the good work. Let all your actions be animated by motives of virtue, by the view of an end the most perfect, which will joyfully and speedily urge you forward; let a pure intention animate you, and continue your work in such a manner that it may be entirely proportioned to the idea which you have formed of perfection. Your proficiency does not consist in the multitude of your exercises, but in the perfection with which you finish the duties of each day. It is not the action, but the manner in which it is done that merits praise.

Your days are flying by, and the past no one can restore to you; your life regards the future more than the present, as it is always hurrying on to tomorrow. Thus your life passes away while you are in the very act of preserving it; meantime, old age comes on apace; so does death, which takes you by surprise, unless you be prepared for it. As a mutual conversation beguiles persons traveling together so that they arrive

sooner at the end of their journey than they
expected, in like manner the different occupations of a distracted mind do not permit you
to perceive your daily journey through life,
which, whether you are awake or asleep, you
make with the same hurried steps, until you
come to the end of it. Why, therefore, do you
delay? Why do you dally? Put a high price on
your time, using it with promptitude and esteeming every day and every hour of it as something
most precious, for its loss cannot be repaired.
You do not suffer anyone to take your farms
from you. A small dispute about boundaries is
enough to make you go to court or take up arms;
and yet you permit everyone to deprive you of
your time and life, than which nothing can be
more precious and of which to be avaricious is
truly honorable.

Recount to yourself your past years, as you
take a review of your life, and you shall see that
although they may exceed one hundred, they
are much less than this number. For how much
time have sleep, good cheer, litigation, friends
and idle gadding abroad consumed? Add to this
the time of which you have made no use and
which escaped you without a thought, doing
nothing, or worse than nothing. You will then
understand how small a portion of time is left,
and you will confess that your death is premature. You will weep for having so often lost the
time which you misspent. Why not strive, then,
to spend the present time in such a manner that

you may be able to say when it is gone by, "I cannot see how I could have employed my time better." The present time consists in a single day, and this day is present with us only by one moment passing after another. Why do you lose this day, which alone is in your power, and plan out the duties of the future, which is not in your power? Delay is the greatest impediment in life. Live today as you ought; it will be too late tomorrow to wish to live.

Let God be the end of all your thoughts, words and actions, excluding every other object from your mind and seeking the accomplishment of His will alone. The man who takes God for his guide never turns aside from the right path. Your affairs shall be in safekeeping if you direct all your actions to the glory of God, laboring as if He alone were looking on, who beholds all, sustains all and governs all. You shall never escape His eyes, for He is present not only to your words and actions, but to your very thoughts, however secret. When you close the doors and cause darkness to succeed light, you should not think you are alone. God, from whom nothing is concealed, makes your secrecy more sacred. *"For in him we live, and move, and are. . . ."* (*Acts* 17:28). In His presence you eat and drink; with Him you walk and treat of your affairs, elevating your being to Him. Make yourself worthy of His regard and love. It is necessary that you be a man of uprightness, for you act before the eyes of your judge, who sees all things. Live as if there were but God and yourself alone in the world. Embrace willingly everything that His providence has ordained for you, whether it be prosperity or adversity. Do you pray to God? What matters it whether it be by this or that way you come to Him? And would to God that you may one day arrive at this happy end!

Chapter XX

THE ADVANTAGE OF SOLITUDE

On the Advantage of Solitude: The society of the wicked must be avoided. The multitude of worldly vices and what they are. The acquisition of virtue is the endeavor of him who wishes to advance in it. The signs by which we know that we have obtained virtue.

IT IS A convincing evidence of a well-regulated mind—one purified from corrupt affections—to be able to enjoy solitude. As God who is the source of His own beatitude always abides in Himself, so you shall approach near the happiness of God if you learn to live content with yourself alone. And indeed you need never be alone, if you wish, provided you make Jesus Christ your companion. But if you have a violent passion for talking, speak with yourself; however, be on your guard, lest you be at the same time speaking with a bad man. But do you wish to know what you may be able to say to yourself alone? Say what men willingly say of others, that is, speak evil of yourself. Arraign your vices before yourself, and correct whatsoever you may find worthy of blame in yourself, and you shall never lack a vice deserving of your healing censure.

Hide yourself in your repose, and hide you repose itself. It is a vain ambition to glory in solitude. In order that your bodily solitude may be both agreeable and useful, join that of the mind to it. Steal yourself away from vain occupations, and retire not only from men but from things that do not concern you. Enjoy sweet liberty apart from every creature, and shut out all their images from your heart. Cast away from yourself all anxiety for perishable things, all frivolous thoughts, and attend to yourself and to God in the hidden recesses of your heart. In this silence of the mind, in this forgetfulness and nakedness of all things, is found true rest and tranquillity. It is there you ought to flee, there you ought to hide and to apply yourself continually, for it is in the abandonment of creatures that we find God.

If you wish to be good, flee the company of the wicked. Nothing is so injurious to good morals as to mix in common with worldly minded people. Never do you bring back the same morals from their company which you took there. A weak mind, one that is not yet established in virtue, cannot sustain the shock of worldly vices. We feel no difficulty in doing that which we see many doing. The soft manners of those with whom you live enervate and weaken your morals; the riches of your neighbors excite your cupidity. One example of impurity or avarice is often enough to make you perish. Parents, companions and servants can draw you into depravity.

All things are full of dangers and snares. As soon as we are born, we are entangled in all that can defile the mind or corrupt the heart. Scarcely is there anyone in the world who does not either praise some vice or imprint it in the heart of someone unknown to him. How sweet, how desirable the flight which will take you from places of public resort and the commerce of men to shut yourself up quickly in your own house! All things within are serene and tranquil; all without, clouds and storms. An accident occurs which calls you out; others join you; an assembly is formed which swells into a worldly crowd. Here many excesses are committed, and you who went out good return home full of vices. It is necessary that you should re-enter your solitude to discover the wounds you have received. Return then into yourself as much as you can, lest this multitude, so corrupted, defile you with their errors. The mind which is the less distracted is the more joyous.

Imagine yourself carried to the top of a high mountain. Behold on all sides the miserable appearance of the world, which will teach you to hate it and retire far from it into solitude. You shall see the roads beset with thieves, the seas covered with pirates, wars raging in every place, so as to make the plains wet with human blood, and vice and wickedness, having broken their reins, setting no bounds to their empire. You shall see the impure committing in secret that which does not please even themselves. You shall behold actions so dishonorable and shameful that no one would doubt but that the perpetrators were mad, if only their numbers were few. But the multitude of the foolish being so great has gained for them the protection which the wise deserve. Crime is committed in the very bosom of the law itself, nor is innocence safe where it ought to be defended. The innocent perish, and the guilty are absolved; and this absolution is a greater crime than that which was forgiven. There is no fear of the law, for people do not fear that as an evil from which we can be set free. The tongues of railers are full of bitterness, and the mouths of flatterers deceitful. On one side you see hatred exercising its cruelty; on the other, a compliment full of disguised deceit. One man is gorged with wine, another overpowered with sluggishness. An insatiable avarice takes hold of that man; an ambition (which is the slave of another's judgment) tires out this one.

Behold the multitudes in public places, and you will confess that there are nearly as many crimes as there are persons in them. Almost all sin by their injuries against their neighbor, their contempt of God and their abuse of all His creatures. Being guilty of every crime, they make all things contribute to their own condemnation. And in the midst of so many vices pressing on you from all sides, which overwhelm and sink even him desiring to rise above them and to lift his eyes to Heaven, how shall you be able to stay in the safe path and by calm reflection enter into yourself? It is hard to escape without a wound where the wicked swarm around you, for if they cannot change you, they are at least an obstacle to your perfection. There is only one way of securing sweet repose, and this is to leave the broad road and retire to that position where you can at liberty contemplate the corruption of the world without taking on its contagion. That mind is invincible which, having forsaken external things, devotes itself to its own interior resources and, as if in its own citadel, defends itself. To it the world is a prison and solitude a paradise.

But it is in vain that you separate yourself from men, unless you force the mind to reflect upon itself and betake itself to the practice of virtue. The man who is devoid of virtue has no good quality in him. There is no rest, no happiness but in virtue. In the whole universe, three things concur: God, who is in all and above all; light, which imparts itself to creatures; and virtue, which communicates itself to the perfections of the soul. God is both the light and virtue of all things; light is the ''virtue'' of the material world and the image of God; and virtue is the light of the soul by which we are called and are the children of God. To this concept of virtue you ought to approach with a pure mind if you desire to arrive at the summit of perfection. For virtue is the perfection of man, the renewal of innocence, being replenished with all sweetness. It is the support of nature, which of itself is not capable of attaining to supernatural good. It makes us practice good works with ease, which makes our lives holy, illuminates our darkness and emboldens us to resist sin, to acquire merit and to deserve eternal life. In this endeavor it is necessary to know the nature and action of virtue because no one can love what he does not know. You must then exercise yourself continually in the practice of virtue. And though you should have no occasion of practicing it, still it is necessary for you to imitate the forethought of soldiers, who go through their field exercise before an enemy is in view. Imagine then that you have to struggle against great crimes, that you are overwhelmed with reproaches and that your possessions are violently taken from you; then exercise patience as if all these things had really befallen you. If you thus excite yourself to patience before the day of trouble, you shall not fear when it actually comes. The soldier who has often spilled the blood of the enemy is emboldened with great courage to enter the field of battle.

We cannot gain the habit of virtue except by long practice of it. By these marks you shall know whether you have as yet obtained any virtue: *viz.*, if you perceive that the vices opposed to virtue are extinct, or in a great measure suppressed within you; if you can compel your passions to yield to the bridle of reason and easily obey the mind; if you can with ease, and even with pleasure, exercise acts of virtue; if you despise the sentiments of the tepid and, with full liberty of spirit, boldly do that which displeases the imperfect; if you hate the bad acts to which you had before been the habitual slave; if you do not seem to be delighted with any impurity in your sleep or approve of any injustice; if you strive to imitate that which you praise and admire in others and abstain from those things which you condemn; if you look upon no fault as small and carefully notice and avoid the least imperfections; if you feel neither envy nor displeasure when you hear or see your equals abounding in riches and dignities; if you openly confess your faults, desiring to be reprimanded and corrected for them by all; if, content with the testimony of a good conscience, you cherish the practice of good works and conceal them, for the recompense of a good action is the fact of having performed it; finally, if you day and night labor to gain virtue, for true virtue never slumbers and is always in action.

Chapter XXI

THE THEOLOGICAL VIRTUES

On the Theological Virtues: Good works must bear testimony to our faith. We must place our confidence in God alone. The motives we have of loving God. The love of our neighbor appears in our goodness towards him. An exhortation to alms.

FAITH, without which no one can please God, is the basis of all the other virtues and the foundation of a Christian life. This is the wisdom which has conquered the whole world and to which we must adhere, laying aside all discussion and curiosity. But believe *and* work, because *"faith without works is dead."* (*James* 2:20). Your words and profession proclaim aloud your faith; beware lest your life and morals declare your infidelity. You believe the Gospel— why do you not obey it? You believe in eternal life—why do you not prefer it to the narrow span of your mortal life? To what purpose do you believe things that are true and good, if you be false yourself and work evil? It is an impossibility to form any alliance between true faith and corrupt morals. He alone believes as he ought whose life harmonizes with his faith.

You ought to resign yourself entirely with a

generous and great confidence in God, not doubt-
ing that you shall in His own good time have
the desired aid, since it is most certain that His
providence so disposes and governs all things that
a sparrow cannot fall to the ground, nor a leaf
from a tree, without His permission. Know this,
that the protection of man is deceitful and his
counsels uncertain. Relinquishing, then, all anxiety, commit yourself to the guidance and direc-
tion of God. And if unforeseen accidents,
sickness, calumny or other weightier troubles disturb and interrupt the course of your actions and
designs, do not lose courage, but fortified by
divine hope, give yourself up to God's holy direc-
tion, for His wisdom will lead you out of all those
dangers and conflicts to the end for which He
has destined you from all eternity. Hoping for
the good things to come, man does not feel the
evils of this present time; his power and riches
are commensurate with his hope and faith.

Charity, which is the life and queen of all virtues, concerns God and our neighbor. It is necessary to love God with your whole heart, your
whole mind and with all your powers, above all
lovable creatures, and purely for His own sake
and that of His infinite goodness. Your being, your
life, your motion, your thoughts, your understanding are so many gifts from God. It was God
who redeemed you from the slavery of Satan,
who ennobled your soul with infinite graces, who
prepared eternal life for you without any previous merit. The heavens, the earth, the air, the

water and all things in them daily cry out with
loud voices in order that you may love with great
affection Him by whom all these things were
created for your sake. Why do you go from one
thing to another, seeking goods to be loved by
your soul? Love the one Good in which every
good is contained. Seek this simple Good, which
is the Supreme Good, than which nothing more
lovable can be conceived. It is love by means
of which you can render mutual the affection
which God has for you, although it is impossible
that your love should be equal to His. But charity is not idle; it seeks not its own; and if it be
true charity, it does great things. There is no difficulty which love does not surmount. The true
lover may die, but he cannot be conquered.

Nature has inspired us all with mutual love and
made us for society. We are members of the great
human family and called to the same faith and
glory. He who does not love his neighbor, loves
not God. Now the love of our neighbor consists
in doing good to all, in being useful to all, and
in anticipating the needs of all by kindness and
love. But you ought with a joyful and ready mind
and without any delay—save that caused by the
modesty of him who asks you—give alms to the
poor. The knowledge of their needs ought to be
enough to move you to assist the sorrowful. The
petition, "I beseech you," is painful and bur-
densome. If you anticipate the desire of your
friend when he is going to ask something, you
confer on him a double favor. The person who

receives a favor only when he has asked it does not get it gratis. If you cannot forestall his petition, shorten it, lest you seem to be asked for anything; and with the same good grace show him that you were about to grant his request, although he had not asked it. Then to your good deeds add good words; nor should you mix with your kindness any sadness, unwillingness, reproach or boasting. The favor itself, though you may be silent, will speak for you, and He who sees in secret will reward you.

Among the acts of Christian beneficence, alms-deeds—by which faith is proved, sins are pardoned and Heaven purchased—hold a principal place. Beware, then, lest you despise the poor man whose indigence can make you rich. If you are a slave of your sins, redeem yourself by your money. Out of the instrument of avarice create the benefit of mercy. The stage-player, who only excites your laughter, leaves you with his hands full. Christ offers you the kingdom of Heaven, and you give Him nothing. You pay tribute to your earthly prince, even against your will, although your lands yield nothing; to Christ you refuse a piece of bread out of your superabundance. Take care, lest while you spare your money, you become guilty of your brother's blood. If you do not relieve his hunger, you kill him. You think of leaving others happy after you, but you do not think of your own miserable death. It is much better that your heirs should be deprived of something of your patrimony than that you yourself should lack the means of salvation. Examine your accounts; behold your possessions on earth and those which you may eternally enjoy in Heaven; you shall retain nothing of all your possessions in death save that which you sent before you to Heaven through the hands of the poor. Reproach yourself for your lack of faith. An enemy can invade your house but he cannot assail Heaven.

Chapter XXII

PRUDENCE

On Prudence: Its necessity and difficulty. The method of the prudent man.

PRUDENCE is not less necessary for regulating our actions than the line and level are for executing properly the work of builders. Prudence is the rule of all other virtues, the correct principle of our actions, the eye of our soul and the science of living well. Without prudence, the pleasantness of life is gone. All men say that it is a most difficult art—yes, obscure also. Its difficulty arises first, from the wide range of things, general as well as particular, to which its object extends; and secondly, from the uncertain state of human affairs, for as these are subject to inconstancy and change, depending on many different circumstances, it does not come within the province of every intellect to prescribe a certain rule and temperament by which one might unite and harmonize things so often contrary to one another. Moreover, that darkness which hides from us the reasons and causes of our actions obscures the mind: these causes are like those edifices whose foundations are hidden in the earth, while their spires appear to our eyes. Thus

the divine decrees concerning the prosperous o
unhappy outcome of things are hidden from us
Hence prudence is the lot of only the few, an
only these can foresee what is expedient to b
done in every affair of life.

Prudence takes its origin from experience an
memory, for application and experience enabl
man to understand occurrences that are out o
the ordinary, which prudence then directs. Yo
shall be safe if you rest upon your ow
experience and that of others and do not tak
a position so lofty as to excite your fear o
threaten yourself with a fall. But in order tha
you may prudently dispose all things, you ough
first of all to consider your own powers, the
the business you propose to undertake, and
finally those for whom you must act. Indeed
you must accurately ascertain your own forces
lest you fancy you are able to do more than yo
really can. This man falls in consequence of hi
having relied too much on his own eloquence,
that man, because he did not live according to
his means; another, by overburdening a feeble
body with excessive labors. It is necessary, then,
to estimate the nature of your undertakings and
to measure your strength against them. Only
those burdens are oppressive which are greater
than can be borne. You must undertake that alone
which you can, or at least may hope with cer-
tainty to finish. It is necessary to make a choice
of persons who may be worthy to share a part
of your life. Their morals must be examined, lest

while you endeavor to be useful to others, you injure yourself. Finally, you must reflect whether you have talents sufficient to execute your undertaking and then apply yourself to those duties which you have taken upon yourself. That labor produces no fruit which has to combat the inclinations of nature.

While agitated by his passions, a prudent man undertakes nothing, for the mind, warped and deluded by evil passions, cannot distinguish truth and honesty from what is not. Likewise, that haste which hurries men into great misfortunes from which they cannot extricate themselves is much opposed to prudence; wherefore, the prudent man does nothing rashly, rather subjecting his own judgment to the counsel of others. The thoughts of man are timid, his foresight uncertain, his success doubtful and his experience treacherous. In the counsel of many we find security. Likewise, it belongs to the prudent to strip a thing naked and, without any artificial covering (which is apt to deceive the unthinking), to look carefully into it. Lay aside money, reputation and dignity, and scrutinize the very marrow of the thing itself, examining its nature, not its name. It is foolish to be deceived by mere phantoms and shadows. Then you ought to foresee, as if in a mirror, all that can happen, lest you be forced to utter that foolish expression, ''I did not even think of that!'' To this you must give long consultation, ripe judgment and subtle examination, in order that no adverse circumstance may vitiate your action; nor should your prudence degenerate into cunning and craft, lest finding yourself between a false and a real good, you embrace vice instead of virtue. Lastly, having made your selection, banish all hesitation and execute your decrees with haste. Let your good decision, which cannot be praised except when put into action, suffer no delay.

Chapter XXIII

JUSTICE AND RELIGION

On Justice and Religion: Acts of both. What penance is and in what it consists.

JUSTICE is a noble and excellent virtue which exists not for itself but for others, imparting to them its possession and demanding but one thing only, the exercise of itself. This virtue turns men away from mutual injuries and establishes the world in peace. It is a certain silent convention of nature and the bond of human society; nor can anything be praiseworthy without it. The just man injures no one; neither has he any pretensions to the goods of another; he benefits all, while he thinks and speaks well of everyone; he gives to each his right and does not prevent the good of another. If he command, he orders just things; he is accessible to all and prefers the advantage of those under him to his own benefit. He restrains vice by punishments and crowns virtue with its rewards, and thus his activity embraces all men. If he obey superior authority, he keeps his peace, submits to the laws and orders of those above him, and content with his own state, he does not wish for offices and dignities, nor to burden himself with things which do not belong to him, but he cultivates justice gratis because he considers that there is no greater reward of a just action than to be just.

Religion, the most excellent of the moral virtues, concerns God immediately, His worship and His honor. But the first part of divine worship is to believe in Him and to know Him, then to render to Him the homage due to His majesty and goodness. It is not so much only to know God— the devils themselves know Him and hate Him. To the knowledge of God, then, it is necessary to add charity, or God-like love, and of these two duties (knowledge and love) to make up His worship. And would that they were as well fulfilled as they are known! You know that God is the Great Being who governs the universe, takes care of the human race and manages all things. You confess that He alone is powerful, that He alone is good and that He alone is most high; and you hope in Him as your Sovereign Good and as your final and eternal beatitude. Why, therefore, do you not worship Him as He well deserves? Why do you not give Him sovereign homage? Why do you prefer a little bit of earth to Him? Your religion is vain unless it is recommended by your deeds. Do you wish to be truly religious? Then walk before God and be perfect. In imitating Him you give Him sufficient honor. True religion is that golden chain which unites you to God and God to you. Preserve it unstained from negligence, error and sin. It is a great folly to preach faith with your tongue but infidelity with your morals.

A famous heathen philosopher scoffed at men of this stamp, saying that *there was nothing more glorious than to hear Christians speaking, but nothing more miserable than to see them acting.*

Penance repairs the injury done to God; it inspires the heart with a hatred for sin and is the companion of an efficacious will in satisfying for it. For penance consists in detesting past sin, atoning for it and consenting to it no more. That which once gave pleasure is past; that which accuses, torments and condemns remains forever. What does one gain by hiding his past deformity? There is no guilty person who is not condemned by his own judgment. Nature has established a certain tribunal in the human mind before which each one meets an accuser, a witness and a judge of his crime. Here reflect upon your thoughts and your judgments each day in order to render an account of your actions. Plead your cause before your own conscience and accuse yourself as much as you can. Examine how you have spent the day and, hiding nothing and passing nothing over, measure all your thoughts, words and works. If you acknowledge your iniquity, God will pardon it; if you confess it, you shall be healed. What does it matter that another should know your sins when you yourself are conscious of them? Do you think that it would be more advantageous for you to be condemned in secret than to be absolved in public? In whatsoever place you hide yourself you always carry your conscience with you, nor can you ever flee from it. If you despise your conscience, you are the most miserable of all men.

Our life may be divided into three periods: the present, the past and the future. The present is a moment which vanishes before it comes. The future is not as yet arrived, but your past days shall present themselves to you when you command them to do so and will permit you to consider them as much as you please. You should not fear your memory nor blush to cast your eyes on the past and to reproach yourself for your faults. The more frequently you do this, the more quickly you shall amend. Take vengeance on yourself, and do not commit anymore that which you have wept to have committed. Many, having escaped from ship-wreck, took occasion to forsake forever their ship and the sea, in order to honor the goodness of God who had delivered them, remembering the danger that they had escaped. I wish that you might take great care of yourself, lest you undergo again that which you once had reason to fear. You have escaped great danger; you should not run the risk anymore of perishing. God has spared you as many times as you have sinned. Take care lest the goodness of God be turned by you into an occasion of your becoming a greater sinner. You reflect sometimes on what you are going to do; why do you not reflect on what you have already done? For we take counsel from the past—how to direct us in the future. Many people would have become wise if they had not fancied that they were so already. Unless you daily amend, you shall daily become more sinful.

Chapter XXIV

PIETY AND RESPECT

On Piety and Respect: Obedience and gratitude are commanded. How we are to receive and return a kindness.

THERE IS NO language strong enough to praise the man who can say, "I have always obeyed my parents; to their commands, whether just or severe, I have been compliant and submissive. As to my country, I have always given evidence that I have been a good citizen. I have never ceased to do good to my brothers and relations, and by the force of kindness, I have endeavored to gain the whole world." Truly, these are the works of piety, by which we render due service to our country, parents, brothers and all others united to us by the ties of flesh and blood. But this same piety teaches us to respect prelates, princes, masters and others who in any way surpass us in dignity, wisdom, age, religion and sanctity. For in their presence we are accustomed to rise up, uncover our heads, leave their way, dismount from our horse or carriage, go on our knees, kiss their hand or garments and show other signs of honor according to the custom of the country. All these things indeed you will do with a mind full of respect if you conceive a just estimate of their elevation in life, for this shall produce in your will a certain distance and fear, which will prevent too much familiarity with them; and thus, from the view of their grandeur, you will retire into your own littleness. All power is from God. Whatsoever respect you pay to superiors will always be within just bounds if you regard God in their persons.

As every calamity can be traced back to the disobedience of our first parents, so we are brought back to lost happiness by imitating the obedience of the Son of God. Obedience is the perfection of all things—that which unites them most firmly to their first principle. From God it leads all things in an admirable circle back to God again. Christ, who chose rather to lose His life than to be disobedient to His Heavenly Father, praised it above all other virtues. This virtue is said to be better than sacrifice, because by obedience a person immolates his own will. Without calling into question the cause or motive of the command of a superior, we ought to receive it as a voice from Heaven. He who has perfectly learned to obey passes no judgment on the thing commanded to be done, saying, "Let my superior advise me; let the law order and say what it wishes me to do; I shall not question it, dispute it or excuse myself; but I shall simply obey, prepared to execute with joy and promptitude all things easy or difficult." There is only one case in which you may be disobedient and obstinate, which is this: when anyone attempts to draw you from virtue and make you violate the law of God. In all other things you ought to obey with constancy and without murmuring.

Gratitude is concerned with that which is due on account of a favor received. It is a duty which is indispensable in order to value a benefit, if not according to its magnitude, at least with a view to the sentiments and affections of the donor. Then we ought never to lose the memory of the favor, which should always remain fresh on the mind. No one can be grateful for what he forgets. But he who remembers it has already recognized it. The whole world can do this, since it does not require riches or labor or happiness: under all circumstances, gratitude can promptly show itself. If your resources fail, your will shall not, for it can bear your gratitude to the thrones of kings. When anyone makes you a present, receive it cheerfully, showing your joy, that the giver may see it, and thus reap the first fruits of his own gift. It is a just cause of joy to see a friend joyful, but it is a greater subject of joy to be the cause of it. The man who willingly received a present and is grateful for it has already paid the first interest on it. That man never wishes to be grateful for a favor who casts it so far away from him that he loses sight of it. On the other hand, he has already returned the favor who extolls it and denies that he is able to return sufficient thanks: but he that receives it with disdain and negligence seems to slight it. The man who scarcely shows that he has felt a kindness, with difficulty opening his lips to return you thanks, manifests more ingratitude than if he were altogether silent. The good man returns thanks as soon as he receives a favor. For what is more contrary to your duty than not to restore what you have received? Nor must we restore with the same measure, but with one more copious, just as the earth makes a more ample return of the seed sown in its bosom. Take care, however, lest you be in too great a hurry in returning thanks. Some, as soon as they receive a gift, send you back another in such haste as to show they owe you nothing. This is a certain way of rejecting a present, as by one gift they quickly efface the memory of the other.

Chapter XXV

TRUTH AND ITS USE

*On Truth and Its Use: Simplicity and fidelity
are praised and recommended.*

LET *Truth* be found in all your words,
gestures, writings and other external signs.
Lying lips are unbecoming a Christian man. To
think one thing and to say another is a vice
both effeminate and base. A generous man
announces things as they are, without exaggeration, amplification, deception or dissimulation,
avoiding all equivocation and concealment. Simple truth loves simple words. It exhibits all things
naked, because it is innocent. But the liar and
deceiver, in order to hide a deed, obscures it
by his double-tongued words. The evil speaker,
as well as the evil doer, hates the light. Beware,
therefore, lest you change your sentiments as
you do your dress, having some for your use
at home and others for the public. Let not the
expression on your countenance give the lie to
the truth hidden in your heart. Nature itself
has a horror of this vice. Behold little children
not as yet arrived at the use of reason placing
a lie in the category of the greatest reproaches,
and though they may fall into it by their levity,

nevertheless, they condemn it by the natural rectitude of their judgments. This makes us admire the providence of God, who has implanted virtues in the mind, without which life and society could not exist. But of all lies, that which you commit by the actions of your life is the most pernicious. For if you have a horror of any falsity in words as unworthy of an exalted mind, why do you not dread to be yourself a living lie that endures your whole life? It is something truly great and worthy of admiration for a man to be always the same by uniformity of life and action.

Simplicity is a virtue little known to men. Its excellence is great and much to be praised, since God is exceedingly delighted with it, for *"his communication is with the simple."* (*Prov.* 3:32). Wherefore, since He is most simple and sincere, He desires those souls who come to Him to be simple likewise. Now, that man is simple who does not depart into contradictory ways and who, without any duplicity or hypocrisy, shows himself outwardly as he is interiorly, who when an occasion offers, candidly and sincerely confesses his faults; who is an infant in malice and abhors all the false reasons of worldly actions; and who, without renouncing the rules of prudence, believes each person to be faithful and sincere and does not suspect evil of anyone. It gives him no trouble to appear foolish in the eyes of men, provided he be wise in the sight of God. Estranged from all duplicity, he does all things with the simple intention of pleasing God. O unhappy craftiness! Why are you troubled about many things? *"But one thing is necessary"* (*Luke* 10:42), and that is that you come to Him whose essence is unity and simplicity. Never shall you arrive at this blessed goal if you walk in a duplicitous manner.

Fidelity is numbered among those goods which are the most important to the human race. For, destroy fidelity, and commerce is ruined, friendship dissolved, treaties made void and a whole realm disturbed. However, fidelity is a virtue most rare and, indeed, almost unknown to the world. Behold the number of witnesses employed in contracts, the precautions observed to secure the promises of parties, the care taken in bargains to make them binding, but all of which, nevertheless, are scarcely sufficient. All these show that the great flood of human perfidy has spread far and wide on all sides. Most men are so sordid that in their eyes, gain is more sacred than fidelity. Oh, avowal of fraud and wickedness that ought to cover the human race with confusion! We believe no one without a witness and a surety. We find it safer to rely on parchment than on the sanctuary of the rational soul. But the faithful man always executes his promises; he betrays not the secrets confided to him, observing good faith even to an enemy, and he prefers it to kingdoms and to life itself. He is slow in his promises because he knows that hasty repentance follows hasty promises.

But if once he promises, he neither deceives you nor violates his treaty—unless perchance the nature of things change or he be in danger of falling into sin. A promise which cannot be kept without sin is binding on no one.

Chapter XXVI

FRIENDSHIP

On Friendship: The means of sustaining it. Certain rules for conversation.

NOTHING is more necessary to human life, nothing more profitable, nothing more pleasant than friendship. It is that mutual benevolence of two persons which is founded in virtue and cemented by the sharing of good things. How great is this blessing when the hearts of friends are so happily disposed that every secret finds a safe resting place in one's friend, whose conscience you may fear less than your own, whose discourse calms your anxiety, whose counsel ensures success to your affairs, whose cheerfulness dissipates your sadness and whose looks alone delight you? What is more delightful than a friend to whom you need not fear to reveal your faults and whose deportment itself is advantageous? When certain small insects wound only your skin, you do not feel them, their force being so delicate and subtle, and it is only by the swelling which follows that you know they have bitten you. The same thing happens to you in the conversation of a good friend. You shall not be able to discover how and when he befriended you until afterwards. But true friendship cannot exist unless mutual affection intervenes; however, the principal part of that twofold affection is to love rather than be loved. Benevolence, then, is the foundation of friendship, whose mutual love is the end it has in view. Likewise, true friendship, of which Christ is the sacred bond, is not founded on the interest of earthly goods, on the sole presence of anyone, on empty compliments or deceitful flattery, but on the fear of God and the study of divine learning.

Great care is necessary in the choosing of a friend. According to a popular proverb, "We must eat many measures of salt before we can contract a perfect friendship." Now there are four things which must recommend him whom you intend to choose as your friend: *Fidelity*, which is hard to find and whose shadow scarcely appears on earth, that you may commit to his safekeeping yourself and all belonging to you; *intention*, that his friendship may have an upright object in view and that divine things may not degenerate into baseness; *discretion*, in order that you may know what you ought to give your friend and what you ought to ask of him; *patience*, that his heart may be prepared to suffer any adversity for a friend. Having discovered these qualities in your friend, you ought, moreover, to find out how he treated his former friends, for you may expect that his conduct to you will be the same as that which he showed to others. A faithful friend is a living treasure.

Our care in keeping him ought to be equalled only by our grief in bewailing him when gone. You may be pronounced happy if you possess a friend who does not love your riches, your table or the quality of your mind—one who corrects you when you go astray, who supports you when you are going to fall and who encourages you when you are running in the path of virtue. His equal you shall not find under Heaven. There are many who are called friends, but we can count only a few of them who are so in reality. Almost no one loves another without some interested motive. He is by no means a true friend who proposes only himself or external things as the end of his friendship. He will be very fond of you as long as you are useful to him. And as soon as your table is empty, he disappears also, and thus he finishes as he began. You will find the least true friendship where you imagined it was more abundant.

As the physician who is anxious to heal a patient most dear to him spares neither metal nor fire, so ought you to behave towards a friend in need of brotherly correction, acting with the greatest freedom, boldness and firmness, without neglecting or dissimulating anything. That obsequiousness which fosters vice is damnable. But though your admonition be secret, let it be tempered with the greatest sweetness and devoid of all harshness. Reflect a long time before you admit anyone to the number of your friends, and when you resolve to receive him, let his recep-

tion be accompanied with great affection. Speak
to him with the same freedom as you would to
yourself. Indeed you ought to live on such terms
with him as to have no secret which you may
not be able to confide to an enemy. But because
some things happen which custom has made
secret, you should not confide those with your
cares to any but your friend. Some people tell
everyone they meet matters which ought to be
mentioned to their friends alone, and thus they
pour out their troubles into every ear. Others
again there are who, dreading even the conscience of their dearest friends, lock up every
secret in their own breast and if possible would
not confide it even to themselves. But these two
classes of persons are in error: the one thinking
to be more honest, the other more secure; but
if you wish to talk to all without danger, this
you can easily do, not by hiding what you may
have done, but by doing nothing which you may
wish to hide.

Affability has a certain connection with friendship. It is that which regulates conversation in
which we must observe modesty and silence. An
upright man may hear many things, but he says
only a few. It is a contemptible inclination to
wish to be known rather than to know, to make
a useless show of one's advantages rather than
to acquire those which we see in others. You
ought to accustom yourself to the conversation
and moods of those with whom you live; and
because many speak things that are false, fool-

sh, puerile and not at all to the purpose, of all these take no notice. It is the part of a base and ffeminate mind to converse only with those who re complying in their manners and who are eady to applaud and flatter others. Speak sparngly of yourself and of your affairs, nor cling bstinately to your opinion, and abstain from hose proud words which show forth your uthority and superiority. When you meet anyhing unseemly, returning into your own mind, uestion yourself whether you yourself might not ave been guilty of a similar fault. Then, out f all you hear and see, gather a selection that vill suit your progress in virtue. You will do well f, from another's sin, you learn to amend your wn.

When you witness anything strange, unexected and foreign, you should not at once condemn it, for it is only a person of an ill-bred mind hat wonders and scoffs at what is contrary to he customs of his own country. We must judge hings not according to their appearance, but ccording to their reality. Most people rest their esteem of things on their novelty, artifice, rarty, difficulty, show, reputation and exterior ppearance; the wise man looks only to the ntrinsic value and beauty of them and disdains ll those things that the common people admire. You should reap fruit from everything that happens and set no bounds to your progress. With egard to earthly affairs, it is necessary that you put on a mask, so to speak, and imitate the actors of a comedy, who because they portray the life of another person, weep without feeling grief, buy without possessing anything, command without authority, suffer insults without any resentment and who insult others without exciting anger. Would to Heaven that in worldly affairs you would conduct yourself without passion and interest. The world is a great theater in which there are as many actors as there are men, but take care that you be as much as possible a spectator and not an actor in the comedy. Those who have to act a part of the scene must exert themselves much, but the spectators have nothing to do but laugh and entertain themselves.

Chapter XXVII

GENEROSITY

On Generosity: Its definition and how we are to exercise it. In what respect it differs from munificence.

I CANNOT call that man generous who seems angry with money, not knowing how to give or how to keep it, but throws it away rather than bestows it. He is a generous man who gives his money with weight and measure, as he keeps in view the rules of beneficence in his gifts, dispensing them according to his abilities in the proper time and place and on the persons who need them, without looking for any advantage, save that of his neighbor. Generosity is a virtue whose hands are occupied in distributing gifts. Indeed, it consists in receiving as well as in giving them, which is nonetheless its principal office, because *"it is a more blessed thing to give, rather than to receive."* (*Acts* 20:35). When the means of bestowing gifts shall fail, the will of doing so will suffice; and this is the most considerable part of this virtue, for we must not only benefit others but *wish* to be beneficial to them. No one returns thanks to the rivers and the sea which waft our ships, nor to the winds that are favorable to us, because

151

though these things are beneficial to us, they lac
the will of being so. The promptitude with whic
you do a good act to anyone gives a value to you
generosity. Some destroy the grace of their goo
deeds by doing them with distorted faces or pu
ting them off from day to day. Thus they tire ou
the patience of their friends by their delays, as we
as torment them by long expectation. And whil
it is the characteristic of him who gives voluntar
ily to give promptly, he who refuses his gifts fc
a long time does not give with a good grace. A
true generosity runs to meet us, and its gif
becomes the more pleasant as it anticipates ou
petition.

That man cannot live a happy life who only con
siders himself and turns everything to his ow
advantage. You must live for others if you wish t
live for yourself. Why do you cling to things as i
they were really yours? You are but the procura
tor of them. Nothing of these things belongs to yo
which you shut up with iron bars, which you coul
not have possessed without perhaps having in som
way contributed to taking the life of their forme
owners and which you are now ready to defen
with your own. They have only been deposite
with you and are already about to pass into th
hands of another master. An enemy or a hostile suc
cessor may raid them. Do you seek how you sha
make them your own? It is by giving them gener
ously to others. What is it that has given you th
reputation of being a "rich" man? A small house
a little money and a small piece of land. If you ac

nerously toward your neighbor, this will be an
t of beneficence, a virtue which shall remain
ith you forever. Money is not precious except in
s ceasing to belong to you by acts of generosity.
Since great things cannot be done at small
xpense, *munificence* regulates great expenses,
st as generosity does those which are small.
hese two great virtues, so much alike, differ in
ne point only: that one appears in small things,
ne other in great. He whose property is small can
e generous, but he alone obtains the praise of
nunificence whose opulence is great. Properly
peaking, the virtue of munificence is seen only
n works worthy of admiration. For if anyone gives
pearl of great value for a sacred purpose, he is
aid to be in a high degree generous rather than
nunificent; but if he employ the price of this pearl
build a temple or any other splendid and admira-
le edifice, he is called munificent. But the build-
ngs in which great expenses are required are those
vhich belong to the worship of God, the use of the
eople, the jubilee of the public and certain offices
n which men are obliged to acquit themselves in
style of grandeur. In these things a certain
lecency must be observed, both on the part of him
vho makes the expense and with respect to the
xpense itself. He cannot be called munificent
vho expends more than he can afford and who
nvolves himself and his family in debt in order to
ain the praise of being thought munificent. That
nan is truly generous and munificent who takes
rom himself alone what he gives and expends.

Chapter XXVIII

FORTITUDE

*On Fortitude: Its functions. The man who ha[s]
this gift scorns death.*

SINCE man has but little courage and h[is]
nature is weak, fortitude is necessary t[o]
strengthen him, lest terrified by dangers, h[e]
depart from the path of rectitude. The role [of]
fortitude is twofold: The first is to sustain labo[rs]
and dangers, and this is its chief duty; the se[c]-
ond has for its scope the wide field of actio[n]
when it is necessary to engage in it. The ma[n]
invested with the armor of fortitude does no[t]
rashly go to meet misfortunes, but when the[y]
come, he sustains them with constancy. He doe[s]
not look for dreadful things, but he disdains the[m]
when he has to face them. He is elevated wher[e]
others are beaten down; he remains standin[g]
where others have fallen flat to the ground; nei[-]
ther dishonor nor repulse nor exile nor injurie[s]
can subdue him; nor can prisons nor torment[s]
nor death itself strike him with dismay. By vir[-]
tue of his fortitude, he walks in triumph ove[r]
afflictions, maladies and all the trials that befal[l]
him. He permits neither threats nor entreatie[s]
to turn him aside from the path of justice; nei[-]

154

ther does he lose courage, although many obstacles oppose his just designs. He neither yields to his burden nor debates whether he ought to discharge the duties of his office when once undertaken, but he perseveres until he executes his work. Under every weight that presses down upon him, he stands upright, and neither violence nor power nor terror can diminish the force of his energies. The perils that surround him cannot make him flee nor cause him to make shipwreck of his virtue. Heedless of what he suffers, he minds nothing but the object he has in view.

As he who puts to sea, even with a favorable wind, furnishes himself with all things necessary to meet the coming storm, so it is necessary for you, while fortune smiles upon you, to provide yourself with those aids by which you may courageously withstand the shock of adversity. Imagine to yourself that all possible calamities have already befallen you, the loss of things the most dear: shipwreck, exile, wounds, torments, disease, calamity, injuries. And so comport yourself as if you had all manner of misfortunes on your shoulders, in order that, being animated by this preparation, you may be able to say in all events, "I have already had these things before my mind; I foresaw them and disdained them." Whatsoever now gives you joy or pain has been ordained for you from all eternity, and though the life of one person *seems* different from that of another, all must still come to the same end. It is ordained that as we ourselves are mortals, so we have received the inheritance of mortal things. Why then are you sad? Why do you weep? For though all you possess may perish, nothing of your being shall perish. It is much better to give willingly that which God demands of us than to be forced to pay what we owe Him. Epicurus himself has taught that a wise man can be happy even in the midst of torments. If, he says, he were even in the bull of Phalaris,* he would say, "How sweet this is and how little do I care about it." Behold indeed an admirable sentiment, but one not incredible to us among whom so many martyrs have shown such great constancy in tortures and cheerfulness in flames that they seemed not to have felt their torments. All pains are sweet to him who loves God and wishes to suffer them for His sake.

The excellence of fortitude never appears more admirable than in danger of death. It is difficult to lead the mind to a disdain for life—to the love of which most men are wedded and than which they esteem nothing more happy, nothing more precious. But if you be as wise as you ought to be, you will cease to count death among misfortunes, which is actually the *end* of all our miseries and the beginning of true life. You ought willingly to leave that which you shall one day

---

* Phalaris was a cruel tyrant of Agrigentum in Sicily, notorious for shutting up men in a brazen bull and then putting fire under them. He himself perished in this way.

more truly resume. It is only an unthinking person who can fear death, which is by an invincible necessity the lot of all, for we normally fear only those things that are uncertain, while we *expect* things that are certain. Consider that neither infants nor the insane fear death. Indeed, it is a shame if the use of reason cannot bring you that security to which even the absence of reason leads others. Life has been given you on this condition, that you surrender it into the hands of death. The man who does not wish to die really does not want to live.

God bestows on us the favor of using for a time those goods which form such a grand spectacle around us. But as soon as this time is expired, we must leave them all behind. What wise man is there who, having given his last sigh on earth, would wish, if allowed to return to this life again, to occupy once more the prison of his mother's womb, resume the foolish things of infancy, the fears of childhood, the perils of youth, the cares of manhood and the hardships of old age? No one has lived so happily in this world as to wish to be born a second time. Consider, then, where you are speedily going and what things you are leaving behind. You cannot fear the idea of leaving this life if you have a well-grounded hope of entering another that will be far, far better. But behold the cause of your fear: your hands are empty of good works, the desire of which now, at the end of your days, begins to trouble you. Otherwise, you should, while on the very threshold of an eternity of happiness, have no reason to tremble. If the just man were never to die, he would consider his life to have been a punishment!

A man cannot receive death with joy unless he has prepared a long time for it. Make it familiar to yourself, then, by careful meditation, that when it comes, you may meet it with peaceful resignation. A long life consists not in a multitude of days or a number of years, but in the ardent desire of a soul wishing to leave the body and return to its First Principle. He who dies happily has lived a long life, and a good death is the recompense of a good life. Do you desire to prepare for a happy death? Accustom yourself to view all things as beneath you, and disdain them. That man cannot fear death who has already deprived himself of more things than it can snatch from him. Do you wish to make life sweet and agreeable? Lay aside all anxiety for it. Prepare yourself for death in every form; then it should not concern you whether the thread of life shall be cut by the sword or by fever. Live in such a manner that you may be able to say each day, "I have lived." That person's life is secure and his death joyful who, mindful of the tomb, directs all his days to that end and who is privileged truly to live *after* his death. You shall not be able to live truly well unless you die each day.

Chapter XXIX

MAGNANIMITY

*On Magnanimity: The description of a man
emboldened by it.*

MAGNANIMITY, even in its name, implies
something great. It is an elevated virtue
whose power is truly surprising and whose object
is always numbered among things which are the
most sublime. Without this virtue, the efforts
of all the others would fall fruitless to the
ground. For since many obstacles occur in the
exercise of those other virtues, the soul ought
to be raised up and, becoming more courageous
as it marches against them, never rest until all
the interposing difficulties be removed and it
has nobly reached the possession of the desired
good. Magnanimity confers this blessing on man,
as it disposes him always to aim at great and
heroic actions; and relying on the aid of divine
grace, it securely and promptly undertakes the
most difficult enterprises. It is necessary for you
to have courage if you wish to become anything!
Great things are not accomplished by small exer-
tions. Man is a noble creature when he truly
acts the part of man.

A man who has a great mind aspires always

to great things and disdains all those things as nothing which most people desire as great advantages. Truly, he does actions worthy of much honor, but he has no ambition to gain that honor when it is refused to him, just as he disdains it when it is offered to him. If the honor of God and obedience did not order it otherwise, he would do nothing worthy of applause. He performs nothing for the sake of ostentation, but does all in accordance with the laws of his conscience and looks for the reward of his good deeds, not from the approbation of the people, but in the performance of the deeds themselves. He always stands on high ground, a spectacle to the whole world, invincible, equal to himself in every state and fortified with his own greatness. Being the master of all things below him and around him, he submits to no one, petitions no one, because he needs nothing outside himself. Nothing can terrify him or cast him down. In making himself known, he does not wish to become public for the love of vanity, but for the sake of the dignity to which he is elevated and the gifts of God which shine in his person. Meantime, he joins to this elevation the most perfect humility—which remains unshaken before God—because he attributes all his goods and all his glory to Him alone, knowing this with certitude: that he has nothing, can do nothing and is nothing in and of himself. To have the most profound sentiments of humility about oneself and about his advantages is to know the landmarks of virtue. However, without violating the laws of modesty, he need not repudiate the honors which sometimes arise from those advantages. We may let glory follow us, but we can by no means seek for it.

The man who is gifted with magnanimity receives all the assaults of his enemies without turning his back on or resisting them. While he observes due modesty and moderation to persons of the middle and more humble classes, he does not throw himself at the feet of princes and the rich; neither does he flatter them nor suffer their power to oppress his liberty of spirit. He lets all see his disdain for or love of those things which, respectively, deserve them, and he speaks and acts as he ought, because he neither hopes for nor fears anything on this earth. His actions indeed are those of other men, but they are done in a far different manner, and therefore he discloses not his holy intentions to the many and does not lightly mix with other people. Past injuries he does not remember, and he neither complains of nor petitions against those which necessity obliges him to bear. He praises only a few, but he himself desires the praise of none; nevertheless, he does those things which are worthy of praise. He is independent of everyone who is neither his friend nor his superior. His admiration is not easily excited, since nothing earthly seems great or novel to him. Being safe within himself, no accident, no event can move him. His step is slow, his voice grave, his discourse solid and sedate, for he who desires only a few things need not hurry himself, and the person who is content within himself has no necessity of acting with emotion.

Chapter XXX

PATIENCE

On Patience: Its occasions and effects. The signs of true patience. An admonition to bear all kinds of evils. The necessity of perseverance.

PATIENCE is a virtue by which we sustain the evils of this world with tranquillity of mind, but as these evils are many, so patience assumes different names according to the various evils it has to bear. *Patience,* properly so called, supports injuries with fortitude. It is called *equanimity* when it is engaged in bearing the loss of external goods; *longanimity* when it fortifies the heart against the vexations arising from the delay of some dear object long expected; *constancy* when it strengthens the will to bear up under evils of every kind, whether our own or those of others, whether private or public. There is no virtue for whose exercise more frequent occasions occur than patience. For so many troops of evils rush upon us, so many enemies besiege us, that it has been well said, *"The life of man upon earth is a warfare."* (*Job* 7:1). Scarcely a moment passes in which we are not called to the combat. And when there is no external enemy in view, everyone finds enough to contend with in his own breast. All those things which torment and exercise us find their origin in ourselves.

We began our life in tears, not having been able to do anything but weep. This is the first lesson we learned and that which we continue to practice until we die. Some people have passed their entire lives without having once truly laughed; none without having wept. Patience, therefore, is necessary to fortify our heart, strengthen our spirit and perfect our other virtues. No one who is not exercised in the crucible of tribulation can know his own resources. And a man's wisdom is in exact proportion to the extent of his patience.

It would be a misfortune for man should he never know any adversity. Physicians say that nothing is more to be dreaded than too high a state of health,* and sailors look with suspicion upon a dead calm. If calamity inflicts its blows upon you and tears you to pieces, you have indeed entered upon the field of battle, but not upon a scene of cruelty. Unless you fight, you shall never conquer; and unless you conquer, you shall never triumph. But *"Ought not Christ to have suffered these things, and so to enter into his glory?"* (*Luke* 24:26). Can you presume without any tribulation to become the partner of His

---

* This opinion may have been common in the 17th century, but in the modern perception of health, one can never become too healthy. Philosophically and scientifically, "too healthy" is a contradiction of terms. —*Publisher*, 1995.

happiness? You are much deceived if you imagine that you can mount by any other way to Heaven. The whole secret of virtue consists in doing good and suffering evil. And the signs by which we know that we have acquired patience are the following: to suffer evils with constancy from whatever side they come, to abstain from murmuring against God when He chastises us, to avoid fleeing from the company of those who make us suffer, to be guarded against hatred in the midst of reproaches, ascribing all our sufferings to the will of God, who knows what is best for us, to be silent in misfortune, to love those who bring them on us, and to complain to God alone of our injuries, offering ourselves to Him, being ready to endure with joy and thanks all kinds of afflictions. Finally, he is known to be truly patient who shows no impatience at the imperfections of his neighbor.

When you suffer the loss of external goods, it is a great comfort to reflect that the nature of these goods is deceitful and treacherous and that all external things you possess and love have a tendency to flight. These things are indeed in your possession, but they do not belong to you. Do not deceive yourself then by desiring an ownership which in the final view is only imaginary. There is no constancy for him who is a subject of inconstancy; for us who are liable to corruption, nothing is eternal except virtue. Virtue, this one immortal good alone, is all that mortal man can truly possess here below! All the rest carry death with them. Give then such a place to those earthly goods which you have that there may be a great distance between you and them. Nothing can be taken from the good man because he possesses nothing as his own. Why do you sigh for the loss of a little money, the death of a son or the burning of a house, but do not weep for the loss of modesty, of shame or of courage? These indeed are goods that are yours and in your power. Those others are not goods, nor do they really belong to you. If you afflict yourself over their loss, you make it appear that you deserved to lose them. If you loved nothing too much, you would feel that you had lost nothing. The wise man is not afflicted about these external things because they do not concern him.

When you wish to undertake any affair, consider its circumstances. You shall find many things that would trouble your mind had you not foreseen them. Do you call a servant? He may quickly obey your orders, or he may not. Do you wish to visit someone? It may happen that he has retired, that his doors are closed and that he does not want to see you. Foresee these things as possible, and nothing distressing will befall you. But soft and delicate people who never reflect beforehand on what they do will complain: "He would not receive me today, but he received others; he disliked my conversation and left me to the last." The man who realizes that all these things are but the normal tributes of this life is not affected by them and takes no notice of them.

But to endure with patience what you cannot amend is the best course. If anyone through malice or impertinence should offend you, think within yourself whether it be possible to banish all the wicked and impertinent people from the face of the earth; but if this cannot be done, what is so strange that such bad characters should act according to their custom? Take care lest you yourself deserve reproof for not having foreseen the bad practices of those men. The world has always been the same, and wheresoever men are, there are their vices also.

When you feel any pain, do not think about what you suffer, but about what you may have done to deserve it. If you will speak the truth to yourself, you will confess that you deserve greater chastisements than those you endure. God is ultimately the Author of all that happens to you. It is He who wounds in order to heal, who exercises you in order to make you insensible to pain and to prepare you for Himself. He reserves future evils for those whom He now spares.* If you abound in riches, how shall I know the degree of courage you shall have in poverty? If you have grown old amid the plaudits of the people, who will tell me that you shall have sufficient constancy to suffer their affronts and hatred? I have heard that you console others in trouble. I wish you knew how to console yourself and prevent the causes of your own grief.

---

* Cf. the footnote on pages 93-94.

When your physician scars or cuts your members, you both thank him and pay him for it. Why do you not cordially accept the remedies of God? It is madness to mistake those remedies for misfortunes. If poverty, sickness and other things which you call misfortunes had tongues to remonstrate you with, they would reproach you and say, "O man, why do you regard me with horror? Is it on my account you should be deprived of any blessing? Is it I that would injure you, or is it not rather prudence, justice or fortitude that would do so? Is not your joy secure in my company? All these things which you fancy are evils become so many blessings if, undisturbed, you elevate yourself above them. It is indeed a great misfortune not to be able to bear misfortune."

You can sometimes pretend to have resolution in the misfortunes of others, but never in your own. You weep with those who weep, although you have another motive for your tears. Descend from your elevation, and stoop to the afflicted, that you may raise them up. It is necessary indeed to bend oneself to raise that which is on the earth. All things have a twofold handle by which we may hold them; the one is easy, the other difficult. If anyone injure you, be careful lest you deal with him on the side he has injured you, for that would be taking him by the difficult handle; but consider that he was, as well as you, redeemed by the same Blood of Jesus Christ and destined for the same happiness as yourself; this will be taking him by the easy handle. And since friendship is gifted with a very weak voice for free reproof, you should always endeavor to hear your real defects from the mouth of an enemy, who keeps a vigilant eye upon your actions and discovers them more easily than you do yourself. When angry, he reports you through the streets and courts, exposing your hidden faults and those which you yourself neglected to correct. From this conduct learn a useful lesson for your own cure. He takes more care about himself who knows that he has censorious and hostile eyes upon him, always ready to condemn his actions.

Perseverance is the crown and the perfection of the other virtues. A reward is promised to those who begin a virtuous life, but it is given only to those who persevere to the end. Before all things, therefore, stand well with yourself. A thing which benefits us in its passage only is of little use. If you do not advance, you go back; if you only *begin* to stand, you fall. Form your resolution and persevere to the end. It is the nature of an inconstant mind daily to undertake new exercises and never remain in the same position. It is by no means necessary that you should change your place, but it is essential that you perfect your morals. The tree that is often transplanted at last withers; so too, the frequent change of remedies prevents a cure. If the Apostle Paul, a "vessel of election"—regarding not what he had done, but what he ought to have done—was of the opinion that he did not understand himself, what ought you to do, for whom it would be desirable that the end of your course in virtue could be compared to the beginning of his? The love of literature cannot be extinguished by length of years; the desire of riches is insatiable; the thirst of ambition cannot be quenched by honors. We hunt after these finite things without end. But if you taste only lightly the divine wisdom, do you think that you are presently filled? It is not in this manner that He who has called you to perfection has said: *"Be you therefore perfect, as also your heavenly Father is perfect."* (*Matt.* 5:48). Lo, the lofty goal that is prescribed for you, to the end that you should be persuaded that you can and ought always to make new progress in the path of virtue!

Chapter XXXI

TEMPERANCE

On Temperance: How useful modesty is to it. Remarks on abstinence and chastity.

TEMPERANCE regulates those pleasures arising from the senses of taste and feeling. It hates and drives away from it counterfeit and superfluous pleasures; it harmonizes those which are necessary, as much as right reason permits. Its rule is unerring, allowing to the body what is necessary and never seeking pleasure for the sake of pleasure. The object of this virtue is to prevent man from degenerating from the excellence of the human to the baseness of brute nature. It receives great aid from modesty, which is the bridle of depravity, the index of good nature, the guardian of all purity and the witness of innocence. If this virtue becomes mistress of your mind, it will teach you to fear all that is dishonorable, to abstain from every act that is unlawful, to venerate the presence of God, to reverence yourself, to love the intelligent beauty which shines forth chiefly in the works of temperance. Moreover, you shall know that you then have modesty when the very name of intemperance shall make you tremble, when you think that the walls which surround you cannot hide you—far different from those who believe they are surrounded by their house, not to live more securely, but to sin more secretly. But what does it profit you to hide yourself and to flee from the eyes and ears of men? God is always with you wheresoever you are. You cannot separate yourself from your conscience, which accuses you in every place.

Abstinence and sobriety moderate the use of food and drink, while it is the conjoint duty of chastity and modesty to regulate all that regards the sense of feeling. In the use of food, it is very difficult not to be carried beyond the limits of necessity. The innards have no ears to listen to precepts. They demand, cry out and enforce their tribute for each day. Very few think how little is necessary to remove their promptings and satisfy their necessary demands. We compel nature to make itself the slave of vice, employing a rich variety of foods and drinks to excite hunger and thirst, which we can easily appease by ordinary means.

Surrounded as we are by so many temptations to lust, chastity is most difficult to achieve and maintain, unless the fear of God, the flight from dangerous occasions, a watch over the senses and respect for oneself extinguish them. The man who does not respect himself can have no respect for others. Do you wish to be chaste? Set a watch upon your eyes in order that what you accidentally behold without reflection you may not

ccidentally'' love without full and rational con-
nt of the will. Why are you charmed with the
ansitory and false beauty of a creature? Wait
moment, and it shall be no more! Squalid wrin-
es shall plough up that fair forehead; clouds
' sadness shall cover those star-like eyes; and
orrid filthiness shall disfigure those ivory teeth.
ee also the company of the wicked and every
ort of effeminacy, subduing the flesh by fasting
id rigid discipline. He seeks for death who loves
e body to excess, which, in the final analysis,
 the sepulcher of the soul.

Chapter XXXII

MILDNESS AND CLEMENCY

*On Mildness and Clemency: The function a⟩
excellence of both.*

MILDNESS is necessary in order to calm t⟩
violence of anger, that it may not go beyo⟩
the bounds of right reason. Anger furnish⟩
nature with weapons which we may use wh⟨
duty obliges us to reprove and chastise those w⟩
fall into any fault and when prudence tells ⟩
to repulse by just and legitimate means tho⟨
who injure us or a neighbor, lest impuni⟩
encourage the liberty of transgressors. It is ⟨
cruel to excuse all as it is to pardon none. B⟩
when justice obliges you to punish the guilt⟩
remember mildness and mercy. Employ chastis⟩
ments with reluctance, and act in such a ma⟩
ner against sinners as God has acted towards yo⟩
As He has borne with you that He might reclai⟩
you, do you bear with others that they may ⟩
converted. When you despair of the cure of yo⟩
disease, you despise the physician. The facili⟩
of curing the malady of the body is in propo⟩
tion to the skill and good will of the physici⟩
to heal it. The meek man stands in the mid⟩
of the furious waves of passion like a ro⟨

174

evated in the middle of the sea which breaks
e swelling tide, nor does he seek so much the
nishment as the repentance of transgressors.
e Saviour of the world assembled the people
d said to them: *"Come to me, all you that
bour, and are burdened, and I will refresh you.
ke up my yoke upon you and learn of
e. . ."*—not to heal the infirm, nor to cleanse
e lepers, nor to give light to the blind, nor to
ise the dead to life. But for what? *"Learn,"*
e says, *"of me, because I am meek and humble
heart."* (*Matt.* 11:28-29). It seems that He
duced all the treasures of His wisdom and
nowledge to this one thing, *viz.*, that we should
arn to be meek—so great is the excellence of
is virtue.

As mildness moderates anger, so mercy regu-
tes punishment. As mildness regards all men,
mercy belongs to princes and superiors. Its
nction is to award milder punishment to the
fender than the law demands, not through fear,
or interest, nor friendship, nor any other motive,
t through leniency of mind alone. It is not
cessary for the prince to cut off the side of
mountain and build castles in places the most
accessible: mercy is his surest guard; this is his
rong tower which makes his empire secure. A
d prince is hated because he is feared, and
wishes to be feared because he is hated. Now
bjects hate him whom they fear, and people
sire the death of him who is an object of
niversal hatred. Whosoever despises his own life

[e.g., an assassin] is the master of the life of king
In vain does he fortify himself with power wl
finds no security in the benevolence of his su
jects. A great multitude of punishments are :
disgraceful to a prince as many funerals are
a physician. A king shows himself worthy of h
crown when he does not exercise all his powe
when he makes little account of the injuries cor
mitted against his own person, having forgive
that which caused his anger—although justic
obliges him to allow the guilty to suffer fro
the anger of another. It is the characteristic
great courage always to preserve mildness ar
tranquillity.

Chapter XXXIII

MODESTY

*n Modesty: The twofold duty of study. The rule
e must observe in the use of an agreeable and
pleasant disposition.*

MODESTY decks out in great beauty all the
other gifts of the mind. It is the visible face
f honor and the bridle of the vices. Your coun-
enance tells who you are, although your tongue
ay observe silence. The least things serve as
vidence of virtue. The look of a man, his laugh-
er, his gait, the expression of his eyes, often-
mes declare his character. Live then in such
manner that all may know you belong to the
ompany of the Angels. Observe decorum in all
he movements of the body, in your gestures,
oice and looks, lest anything effeminate or flir-
atious, rude or harsh, lurk in them. True mod-
sty reaches from the mind to the body—from
he interior gravity of the one to the surface of
he other—in order that the mind may contem-
late in the body, as in a mirror, its own spiritual
rnaments. The modest man is the living image
f God, for his presence alone stamps modesty
n his beholders. Ah, what advantage is it to
e seen by others, if not in the act of doing good?

178   *Guidance to Heaven*

It is also a duty of modesty to regulate the drap
furniture and ornaments of the house, and t
number of servants, that all may be accordi
to our rank in life. But all these things are or
obstacles and distractions and serve only to orr
ment what is outside yourself. Why then do y
rejoice in your problems? Why do you admi
vanity and glory and a multitude of things th
embarrass you? You may justly call a group
bad servants a hostile army, of which you ca
not be sufficiently on your guard: They wish
know what you do, but not what you comman
There is nothing more humble than the
entrance into your service, nothing more ins
lent than their subsequent conduct, and not
ing more odious than the causes of their leavi
you.

Study has two functions: the first is to mode
ate and regulate the desire for knowledge, whi
sometimes passes all bounds. The second is
banish sloth and rouse the mind to avail itse
of its lights and talents. God, the Author
Nature, has given to man a spirit of curiosit
and being conscious of the beauty and art of H
works, He has made us their spectators, becau
He would have lost all the fruit of His labor
He had no one to admire so much wisdom, gra
deur and beauty as are displayed in them. B
we abuse the advantages of nature when we p
too curiously into things of which it would hav
been more useful to be ignorant. He is not wi
who knows many things, but he alone is wis

who knows the way of doing his duty. You must first learn those things which regard your salvation. I do not object to your learning other things, provided you refer all you read to the perfection of your morals. But beware lest the reading of many books should make you inconstant and unsteady. It is necessary to nourish one's mind at leisure with the doctrine of certain authors if you desire to draw anything from them that will abide faithfully in the memory. A variety of reading delights us, but we can seldom derive any solid advantage except by confining ourselves chiefly to one author.

It is necessary to unbend the mind by mingling rest with labor, for unless we do so, it cannot last long. Legislators have appointed certain days during which the people rejoiced in a public manner, in order that they might receive fresh vigor in their pursuits. But many things contribute to the relaxation of the mind: for instance, a walk in a pleasant and open place, that the mind may be restored and the body refreshed in the pure air; a retreat to a house in the country far from the noise and impure atmosphere of the city; fowling and hunting, if suitable to your station in life; fishing, which is still more innocent; sweet and agreeable occupations, as a concert of music; and some childlike playing; finally, harmless games and merriment, remote from injury and indecency. There are some persons who are too severe—actually haters of their own kind—who, brooding over their own darkness, can never be forced to use a cheerful word. Others again there are who, being always given to jests, never apply themselves to anything serious nor leave worldly society. Now it is necessary to learn how to blend these things and make one succeed another. For solitude causes the desire for company, and company the desire for solitude, one being a remedy for the other. Thus, repose shall heal the dislike for labor, and again labor shall banish the irksomeness of repose. There are persons who, not knowing how to manage their resources, govern themselves without moderation. They lack a system. They do not know when to interrupt their studies or when to resume them again. In applying themselves to their labors, they turn night into day, nor do they cease until they exhaust their strength. Then they give themselves up to amusements and live in such a way that it is with difficulty they can resume their first exercises. We must therefore give such relaxation to the mind that it may be amused but not dissipated. For this it is necessary to have the virtue which the ancients called *"eutrapalia,"* which gave to mental amusements certain limits beyond which it was not allowed to pass. The most excellent things become evils when used to excess.

Chapter XXXIV

HUMILITY

On Humility: In what it consists. Of the knowledge of oneself. The character of the truly humble man.

HUMILITY came from Christ. It was He who taught it by His words and enforced it by His example. After the theological and intellectual virtues, humility holds the first place among the rest. This virtue makes us objects of love and complacency to God, because *He communes with the humble.* In the spiritual edifice there is nothing solid, nothing durable, without humility, which is the foundation of the other virtues. But though from its name it seems to be mean and abject, yet it is the virtue of great souls because it is the virtue of the perfect and it raises the mind to things the most exalted. Humility is most courageous and magnanimous; it soars to sublime and great things, undertaking the most brilliant enterprises without danger of pride and the most difficult labors without fear of opposition. Humility does not consist, as most people think, in simply looking down upon oneself, but in that proper desire for glory and honor which avoids every excess and keeps remote from every imperfection. The humble man desires glory only as the reward of virtue. He does all his actions, not through a motive of vanity, but of virtue alone, to whose dictates he is obedient in every degree of toil. That honor which virtue does not obtain is illegitimate. But because the humble man is gifted with penetration of mind and has a just estimation of his own merits, he therefore is deservedly averse to every honor, as much on account of the little which he realizes he himself has contributed to the practice of virtue, as on account of his fearing that the desire of due honor may carry him to the excess of wishing for that which is not his due. It is much safer then to disdain honor—which is the greater by its having been refused and the more increased by its having been scorned.

You are by no means humble, because you do not know yourself. There is no region of the globe so remote of which you do not more easily believe the most false narratives than you do those things which have been told you of yourself. What is man? His body is fragility itself, unarmed by nature, in need of another's aid and exposed to all the injuries of time. He is but a heap of mud, a filthy animal inclined to all kinds of evils, and in matters of judgment so perverse and depraved that he generally prefers the earthly to the celestial and the perishable to the everlasting. Indeed *"All things are vanity"* (*Eccles.* 12:8)—every man living. There is no animal whose life is more fragile than man's, whose rage is more violent, whose

fear is more dreadful, whose love for sensual
pleasures is more ungovernable than his. O miserable creature, and of all the most unfortunate!
From what source, then, has arisen your pride?
If one spark of reason can be found in you, consider your misery, reflect on your shame and
infamy. Then, knowing yourself, you shall be perfectly humble.

The truly humble man looks down upon himself altogether, nor does he wish to be reputed
as humble, but as unworthy. He gives all honor
to God, to whom all is due, and in all things dis-
trusts himself. He rejoices in his contemptible
state, and in this alone he feels pride because
he disdains all praise. He considers himself with
reference to the things which he has in and of
himself, but others with respect to the things
which they have from God: and thus comparing
himself with others, he concludes that he is worse
than all mankind. For herein lies the genius of
humility: to compare one's own evil deeds with
the good deeds of others. Hence, the most perfect people can, without any falsehood, esteem
themselves the most imperfect of all. Moreover,
the truly humble man submits himself with all
obedience to his superior, giving up his own will;
he discovers willingly his own faults, suffering
with patience all sorts of injuries and embracing
with joy things the most abject in themselves;
he flees from singularity, abstains from any
unnecessary conversation and wishes to live a
hidden life, unknown to the world. He puts all

things beneath himself and himself beneath all things, and shuts himself up altogether in nothingness. Modest and circumspect, he does not speak unless necessity obliges him, and then with modesty and gravity, because he would rather weep than laugh. The carriage of his body marks the humility of his heart. His eyes are cast down, his walk grave and modest, his look like that of a criminal who must appear before the dread tribunal of Divine Justice; conscious of his sins, uncertain of grace and doubtful of his salvation, he dares not raise his eyes to Heaven, but standing afar off like the humble publican of the Gospel, with fervent prayer he implores the pardon of his sins. Finally, he trembles for all his works and disdains all earthly treasures, trampling, so to speak, the pomps of this world underfoot, for he who believes himself to be nothing looks upon the whole world likewise to be nothing.

Chapter XXXV

THE STATE OF THE PERFECT

On the State of the Perfect: The image of the perfect man. The end of the perfect life is to be united with God.

WE PRONOUNCE him perfect who lacks nothing. But what can he lack who, having been purged from his sins, purified from his vices and adorned by all virtues, is intimately united to his God and becomes one spirit with Him forever? Behold the summit of Christian perfection, the last end to which you ought to aspire! A thing is said to be perfect when it is united to its end, the thing for which it was made. But God is your end; it is necessary, therefore, that you should arrive at that final perfection, that, being perfectly united to your Creator, you may thus return to the First Principle of your being. No one, however, can be perfect without the special grace of God. And because not many among mortals dispose the superior part of the soul for receiving the special "overflowing" of the Divinty, so also, few arrive at perfection, and in each succeeding age there are seen but few who are perfect.

That man, you will say, is perfect who is

intrepid in the midst of dangers, without emo
tion while surrounded by objects of passion
happy in adversity and ignominy, calm in the try
ing storms of affliction. Whatsoever others eithe
fear or desire only draws forth his smile, lettin
all things pass by as of minor importance an
applying himself solely to his own spiritual good
He is always in the enjoyment of liberty, alway
faithful to his conscience, always consistent
upright and exalted, empty of himself and fu
of God, a man of whose goods no violence ca
rob him. Evils he turns into blessings. And h
suffers nothing to frustrate his resolves, as h
presses every accident into the service of his soul
He esteems things not according to the commo
opinion respecting them, but according to th
nature of the things themselves. Although he i
in the world, he is always raised above it. Hi
actions are always before his eyes; he is alway
tranquil, always unshaken, as his soul alway
remains with the Principle that gave him exis
tence. For as the rays of the sun, though the
touch the earth, continue nevertheless unite
to the great globe of light from which they ema
nate, so the perfect man converses with us her
below, but his soul is absent from us, being alway
conjoined to the blissful end of his existence. Hi
spirit resembles the state of the firmament abov
the moon, for there perpetual calm reigns. H
is a stranger to the defects of all other creatures
as well as to inconstancy of mind. He makes al
ages work for his good, surveying all equally, a

he sun has done since the birth of time; and
aving far away from himself the multiplicity
f creatures, he reposes in the simple unity of
he Divine Being; nor does he seek anything
utside of himself, having no need of looking
or a happiness which he carries locked up in
is own heart. For God alone he labors, for Him
lone he lives, and for Him he is always ready
o leave this world. As the builder, then, applies
he level to his work, so do you compare your
fe with this chapter, and you shall see how
ar you are from perfection.

This state is too high for you to reach unless
ou are drawn upwards by Him who has said,
'*Without me you can do nothing.*'' (*John* 15:5).
But it is necessary that we should have previous
dispositions. The end purpose of a life of perfec-
ion is to be united to God, and you can never
pproach Him—because He ''dwells in light inac-
essible'' (*1 Tim.* 6:16)—unless you drive from
ourself the darkness of creatures. Man cannot
become a sharer in the Divine Nature unless he
ranscends in mind and affection all earthly
hings. The least attachment which you have is
ike the little fish that the Latins call *Remora*,
which fixing itself to a ship, could stop and hold
t in the middle of its course. Thus it happens
o most persons—who like vessels are laden with
he riches of Heaven and shall happily reach the
harbor of blissful union with God, unless they
be detained on their way by some affection for
vice. For since the nature of God is oneness and

simplicity itself, the soul shall never be capable
of being united to Him if it does not become one
and simple like Him.

*If you have enjoyed this book, consider making your next
selection from among the following . . .*

Miraculous Images of Our Lady. *Joan Carroll Cruz* 20.00
Brief Catechism for Adults. *Fr. Cogan* 9.00
Raised from the Dead. *Fr. Hebert* 15.00
Autobiography of St. Margaret Mary 4.00
Thoughts and Sayings of St. Margaret Mary 3.00
The Voice of the Saints. *Comp. by Francis Johnston* 5.00
The 12 Steps to Holiness and Salvation. *St. Alphonsus* . . 7.00
The Rosary and the Crisis of Faith. *Cirrincione/Nelson* . . 1.25
Sin and Its Consequences. *Cardinal Manning* 5.00
Fourfold Sovereignty of God. *Cardinal Manning* 5.00
Dialogue of St. Catherine of Siena. *Transl. Thorold* 9.00
Catholic Answer to Jehovah's Witnesses. *D'Angelo* 8.00
Twelve Promises of the Sacred Heart. (100 cards) 5.00
St. Aloysius Gonzaga. *Fr. Meschler* 10.00
The Love of Mary. *D. Roberto* 7.00
Begone Satan. *Fr. Vogl* 2.00
The Prophets and Our Times. *Fr. R. G. Culleton* 11.00
St. Therese, The Little Flower. *John Beevers* 4.50
Mary, The Second Eve. *Cardinal Newman* 2.50
Devotion to Infant Jesus of Prague. Booklet 75
The Wonder of Guadalupe. *Francis Johnston* 6.00
Apologetics. *Msgr. Paul Glenn* 9.00
Baltimore Catechism No. 1 . . . . 3.00
Baltimore Catechism No. 2 . . . . 4.00
Baltimore Catechism No. 3 . . . . 7.00
An Explanation of the Baltimore Catechism. *Kinkead* . . .13.00
Bible History. *Schuster* 10.00
Blessed Eucharist. *Fr. Mueller* 9.00
Catholic Catechism. *Fr. Faerber* 5.00
The Devil. *Fr. Delaporte* 5.00
Dogmatic Theology for the Laity. *Fr. Premm* 18.00
Evidence of Satan in the Modern World. *Cristiani* 8.50
Fifteen Promises of Mary. (100 cards) 5.00
Life of Anne Catherine Emmerich. 2 vols. *Schmoger* 37.50
Life of the Blessed Virgin Mary. *Emmerich* 15.00
Prayer to St. Michael. (100 leaflets) 5.00
Prayerbook of Favorite Litanies. *Fr. Hebert* 9.00
Preparation for Death. (Abridged). *St. Alphonsus* 7.00
Purgatory Explained. *Schouppe* .13.50
Purgatory Explained. (pocket, unabr.). *Schouppe* 7.50
Spiritual Conferences. *Tauler* 12.00
Trustful Surrender to Divine Providence. *Bl. Claude* 4.00
Wife, Mother and Mystic. *Bessieres* 7.00
The Agony of Jesus. *Padre Pio* 1.50

Prices guaranteed through June 30, 1996.

Catholic Home Schooling. *Mary Kay Clark* 15.00
The Cath. Religion—Illus. & Expl. *Msgr. Burbach* 9.00
Wonders of the Holy Name. *Fr. O'Sullivan* 1.50
How Christ Said the First Mass. *Fr. Meagher* 16.50
Too Busy for God? Think Again! *D'Angelo* 4.00
St. Bernadette Soubirous. *Trochu* 16.50
Passion and Death of Jesus Christ. *Liguori* 8.50
Treatise on the Love of God. 2 Vols. *de Sales* 16.50
Confession Quizzes. Radio Replies Press 1.00
St. Philip Neri. *Fr. V. J. Matthews* 4.50
St. Louise de Marillac. *Sr. Vincent Regnault* 4.50
The Old World and America. *Rev. Philip Furlong* 16.50
Prophecy for Today. *Edward Connor* 4.50
Bethlehem. *Fr. Faber* 16.50
The Book of Infinite Love. *Mother de la Touche* 4.50
The Church Teaches. Church Documents 15.00
Conversation with Christ. *Peter T. Rohrbach* 8.00
Purgatory and Heaven. *J. P. Arendzen* 3.50
Liberalism Is a Sin. *Sarda y Salvany* 6.00
Spiritual Legacy/Sr. Mary of Trinity. *van den Broek* . . . .`. 9.00
The Creator and the Creature. *Fr. Frederick Faber* 13.50
Radio Replies. 3 Vols. Frs. *Rumble and Carty* 36.00
Convert's Catechism of Catholic Doctrine. *Geiermann* . . . 3.00
Incarnation, Birth, Infancy of Jesus Christ. *Liguori* 8.50
Light and Peace. *Fr. R. P. Quadrupani* 5.00
Dogmatic Canons & Decrees of Trent, Vat. I. 8.00
The Evolution Hoax Exposed. *A. N. Field* 6.00
The Priest, the Man of God. *St. Joseph Cafasso* 12.00
Christ Denied. *Fr. Paul Wickens* 2.00
New Regulations on Indulgences. *Fr. Winfrid Herbst* 2.50
A Tour of the Summa. *Msgr. Paul Glenn* 18.00
Spiritual Conferences. *Fr. Frederick Faber* 13.50
Bible Quizzes. Radio Replies Press 1.00
Marriage Quizzes. Radio Replies Press 1.00
True Church Quizzes. Radio Replies Press 1.00
St. Lydwine of Schiedam. *J. K. Huysmans* 7.00
Mary, Mother of the Church. Church Documents 3.00
The Sacred Heart and the Priesthood. *de la Touche* 7.00
Blessed Sacrament. *Fr. Faber* 16.50
Revelations of St. Bridget. *St. Bridget of Sweden* 2.50
Magnificent Prayers. *St. Bridget of Sweden* 1.50
The Happiness of Heaven. *Fr. J. Boudreau* 7.00
The Glories of Mary. *St. Alphonsus Liguori* 16.50
The Glories of Mary. (pocket, unabr.). *St. Alphonsus* . . . 9.00

Prices guaranteed through June 30, 1996.

Eucharistic Miracles. *Joan Carroll Cruz* 13.00
The Curé D'Ars. *Abbé Francis Trochu* 20.00
Humility of Heart. *Fr. Cajetan da Bergamo* 7.00
Love, Peace and Joy. (St. Gertrude). *Prévot* 5.00
Père Lamy. *Biver* 10.00
Passion of Jesus & Its Hidden Meaning. *Groenings* 12.50
Mother of God & Her Glorious Feasts. *Fr. O'Laverty* . . . 9.00
Song of Songs—A Mystical Exposition. *Fr. Arintero* 18.00
Love and Service of God, Infinite Love. *de la Touche* . . . 10.00
Life & Work of Mother Louise Marg. *Fr. O'Connell* 10.00
Martyrs of the Coliseum. *O'Reilly* 16.50
Rhine Flows into the Tiber. *Fr. Wiltgen* 13.00
What Catholics Believe. *Fr. Lawrence Lovasik* 4.00
Who Is Teresa Neumann? *Fr. Charles Carty* 2.00
Summa of the Christian Life. 3 Vols. *Granada* 36.00
St. Francis of Paola. *Simi and Segreti* 7.00
The Rosary in Action. *John Johnson* 8.00
St. Dominic. *Sr. Mary Jean Dorcy* 8.00
Is It a Saint's Name? *Fr. William Dunne* 1.50
St. Martin de Porres. *Giuliana Cavallini* 11.00
Douay-Rheims New Testament. Paperbound 13.00
St. Catherine of Siena. *Alice Curtayne* 12.00
Blessed Virgin Mary. *Liguori* 4.50
Chats with Converts. *Fr. M. D. Forrest* 9.00
The Stigmata and Modern Science. *Fr. Charles Carty* . . . 1.25
St. Gertrude the Great 1.25
Thirty Favorite Novenas 75
Brief Life of Christ. *Fr. Rumble* 2.00
Catechism of Mental Prayer. *Msgr. Simler* 1.50
On Freemasonry. *Pope Leo XIII* 1.25
Thoughts of the Curé D'Ars. *St. John Vianney* 1.50
Incredible Creed of Jehovah Witnesses. *Fr. Rumble* 1.00
St. Pius V—His Life, Times, Miracles. *Anderson* 4.00
St. Dominic's Family. *Sr. Mary Jean Dorcy* 24.00
St. Rose of Lima. *Sr. Alphonsus* 12.50
Latin Grammar. *Scanlon & Scanlon* 13.50
Second Latin. *Scanlon & Scanlon* 12.00
St. Joseph of Copertino. *Pastrovicchi* 4.50
Three Ways of the Spiritual Life. *Garrigou-Lagrange* 4.00
Mystical Evolution. 2 Vols. *Fr. Arintero, O.P.* 30.00
My God, I Love Thee. (100 cards) 5.00
St. Catherine Labouré of the Mirac. Medal. *Fr. Dirvin* . . 12.50
Manual of Practical Devotion to St. Joseph. *Patrignani* . . 13.50
The Active Catholic. *Fr. Palau* 6.00

Prices guaranteed through June 30, 1996.

At your Bookdealer or direct from the Publisher.

Prices guaranteed through June 30, 1996.